JOSEF VON STERNBERG

PYGMALION AND GALATEA
Sternberg and Dietrich on the set
of *The Scarlet Empress* (1934)

Josef von Sternberg

A Critical Study by

Herman G. Weinberg

A Dutton  *Paperback*

New York
E. P. DUTTON & CO., INC.
1967

To my daughter, Gretchen,
faithful companion of my "thousand and one nights" of filmgoing.

H.G.W.

ACKNOWLEDGMENTS

The author would like to thank the following for their collaboration on this book: Mlle. Michèle Firk and the Messrs. Henri Agel, Michel Aubriant, Peter Balbusch, Kirk Bond, Jean de Baroncelli, Michel Cournot, Philippe Demonsablon, Philippe Esnault, Charles Ford, Robert Florey, Charles Graves, René Jeanne, Ado Kyrou, Andrew Sarris, and Jack Smith. Also, the publishing houses of Éditions du Terrain Vague, Éditions Robert Laffont, and Éditions Universitaires, and the publications *The Bystander, Film Courier, Film Culture, Positif, Cahiers du Cinéma, France-Soir, Paris-Presse, Le Monde, Le Nouvel Observateur,* and the Museum of Modern Art for certain stills from their collection. Also, the Institut des Hautes Études Cinématographiques.

The author wishes particularly to thank Mr. Pierre Lherminier, who supervised the original French edition of this book for Éditions Seghers and for selecting the French critical reviews. Also, Mr. Herbert G. Luft for his help in establishing certain historical facts in connection with Sternberg's Berlin period.

Finally, the author wishes to thank Mr. Josef von Sternberg, himself, for putting numerous documents from his personal archives at my disposal and for checking the factual aspects of the manuscript.

H. G. W.

All notes and translations from the French by Herman G. Weinberg.

TABLE OF CONTENTS

PROLOGUE   *13*

JOSEF VON STERNBERG: A CRITICAL STUDY   *17*

A PERSONAL NOTE   *113*

AN INTERVIEW   *121*

EXCERPTS FROM CORRESPONDENCE   *135*

EXTRACTS FROM SCENARIOS   *141*

   "Shanghai Express"   *143*

   "Anatahan"   *163*

CRITICAL REVIEWS   *177*

FILMOGRAPHY   *231*

BIBLIOGRAPHY   *247*

AUTHOR'S NOTE   *255*

LIST OF ILLUSTRATIONS

Josef von Sternberg and Marlene Dietrich on the set of *The Scarlet Empress* (*frontispiece*)

Sternberg, George K. Arthur, and Georgia Hale on the set of *The Salvation Hunters*   20

Early scene from *The Salvation Hunters*   21

Sternberg, Douglas Fairbanks, and George K. Arthur   23

Scene from the original version of *The Exquisite Sinner*   25

Production scene from *The Exquisite Sinner*   26

Will Hays, Sternberg, Mae Murray, and Robert Z. Leonard on the set of *The Masked Bride*   28

Production scene from *The Sea Gull*   29

George Bancroft, Clive Brook, and Evelyn Brent in *Underworld*   32

Larry Semon and Evelyn Brent in *Underworld*   33

Emil Jannings in *The Last Command*   36

Emil Jannings in *The Last Command*   38

William Powell and Evelyn Brent in *The Dragnet*   40

Clyde Cook and George Bancroft in *The Docks of New York*   42

Sternberg directing *The Docks of New York*   43

Betty Compson and George Bancroft in *The Docks of New York*   44

James Hall and Esther Ralston in *The Case of Lena Smith*   46

Esther Ralston in *The Case of Lena Smith*   47

George Bancroft in *Thunderbolt*   49

Marlene Dietrich in *The Blue Angel*   52

Marlene Dietrich in *The Blue Angel*   53

Marlene Dietrich and Paul Porcasi in *Morocco*   98

Marlene Dietrich and Gary Cooper in *Morocco*   99

Marlene Dietrich and Warner Oland in *Dishonored*   127

Marlene Dietrich and Lew Cody in *Dishonored*   129

Phillips Holmes and Sylvia Sidney in *An American Tragedy*   131

Clive Brook and Marlene Dietrich in *Shanghai Express*   157

Anna May Wong and Marlene Dietrich in *Shanghai Express* 159

Sternberg on the set of *Shanghai Express*   178

Marlene Dietrich in *The Blonde Venus*   179

Marlene Dietrich in *The Blonde Venus*   180

Paul Ivano and Sternberg   183

Sternberg and Marlene Dietrich   184

Sam Jaffe and Marlene Dietrich in *The Scarlet Empress*   189

Louise Dresser, Marlene Dietrich, and Sam Jaffe in *The Scarlet Empress*   190

Detail from *The Scarlet Empress*   191

Marlene Dietrich in *The Scarlet Empress*   192

Marlene Dietrich and Lionel Atwill in *The Devil Is a Woman*   195

Marlene Dietrich in *The Devil Is a Woman*   196

Marlene Dietrich and Cesar Romero in *The Devil Is a Woman*   197

Marlene Dietrich in *The Devil Is a Woman*   198

Peter Lorre and Marian Marsh in *Crime and Punishment* 200

Grace Moore and Franchot Tone in *The King Steps Out*   201

Sternberg on the set of *I, Claudius*   202

Charles Laughton and Flora Robson in *I, Claudius*   203

Emlyn Williams in *I, Claudius*   204

Tom Brown, Wallace Beery, and Alan Curtis in *Sergeant Madden*   205

René Clair, Marlene Dietrich, Joe Pasternak, and Sternberg 206

Gene Tierney and Ona Munson in *The Shanghai Gesture* 207

John Wayne and Janet Leigh in *Jet Pilot*   208

William Bendix and Jane Russell in *Macao*   209

Akemi Negishi, interpreter, and Sternberg on the set of *Anatahan*   219

Akemi Negishi in *Anatahan*   220

Marlene Dietrich, Sternberg, and Herman Weinberg   228

PROLOGUE

Everything is in the human face—all mysteries, all dreams and desires. The character behind the right face for the role reaches you with the speed of light. Compare Gerard van Honthorst's *Dionysus* with Caravaggio's *Bacchus*. It isn't necessary for Caravaggio to depict Bacchus in action doing "a Bacchic thing," as Honthorst is impelled to do by showing Dionysus pressing wine from grapes, to get the point across. Caravaggio does it simply in his portrayal of Bacchus's face. So expressive of the subject is it that he could even have omitted the vine leaves in his hair.

. . .

"In old Canton there once abounded a type of magician called 'bewitchers of the night,' who, with the help of lanterns and Bengal lights, cymbal music, burning incense, sweet nectars and balls of jade, which spectators were asked to rub between their fingers, played on the five human senses until they succeeded in casting their audience into a dream world that turned an ordinary evening into a night of fantasy and revelry."

—DR. FELIX MARTI-IBAÑEZ

"Only one kind of director is dangerous to an actor—the timid guy, the kind guy, the guy who is unsure. A tough guy who knows what he wants is no problem for a pro—you give him what he wants, and that's the end of it."

—PETER USTINOV

"There are no facts, only interpretations of facts."

—NIETZSCHE

"You use 7 people to paint a crowd—not 700."

—DEGAS

JOSEF VON STERNBERG

I

Josef von Sternberg was born in Vienna (at Blumauergasse 25—the house is still standing) on May 29, 1894, of Austrian parents. At seven he was brought to the United States, but subsequently returned to Vienna to attend school. It was there, from Arthur Schnitzler, that he received his first encouragement. He returned to the United States where he eventually found work in the motion picture industry in Fort Lee, New Jersey, as a film-patcher for the old World Film Company, gradually working himself up to cutter, writer, assistant director and, finally, personal advisor to William A. Brady, then general manager of the World Film Company. When the United States entered the First World War in 1917, Sternberg joined the Army Signal Corps and was stationed at G.H.Q. in Washington, D.C., where he made training and indoctrination films for recruits. For his exemplary work he was cited by the War College. Following the Armistice, he embarked on his *Wan derjahre*—a period he terms his apprenticeship—spent in New York, England, and Hollywood, during which he worked with such early directors as Hugo Ballin, Wallace Worsley, Lawrence C. Windom, Roy William Neill, and Émile Chautard.

It was Émile Chautard, the French director, who in 1921 first stimulated the young Sternberg during the filming by Chautard of *The Mystery of the Yellow Room* from the famous mystery novel by Gaston Leroux. Chautard, who had previously won renown as a stage actor (he had appeared with Sarah Bernhardt in Paris), invited Sternberg to watch the players through the camera's view-finder. Chautard showed him how to put objects in front of the camera in their proper perspective, thereby giving every angle a perfect balance. "A long journey begins with a single step," said Lao Tse (echoed many years later by Sternberg in his narration for *Anatahan*). This introduction to "framing the shot" was to become for Sternberg a very long and memorable journey, indeed, as he explored its possibilities, ultimately to become one of the screen's greatest masters of pictorial composition. Sternberg feels that the encouragement given him by Chautard (who was later to appear as an actor in two of Sternberg's films, as the French officer who speaks at the engagement reception of Amy Jolly and LeBessière in *Morocco* and as the dishonored French officer, Major Lenard, in *Shanghai Express*) helped him to a great degree in his determination to pursue his creative aspirations via the cinema.

In 1922 Sternberg found himself in England at the Twickenham Studios with the Alliance Film Company, working with Harold Shaw.

It was in this early formative period that a popular matinée idol of the day, Elliott Dexter, who was the star of a film, *By Divine Right* (1924), on which Sternberg was scenarist and assistant to director Roy Neill, suggested that a "von" be added to Sternberg's name, not only to enhance his screen credit but also to enhance the "artistic prestige" of the picture. "I was ennobled by Elliott Dexter," said Sternberg wryly years later. But the "von" stuck and few aristocrats have carried the noble prefix to their family name with the grace and patrician achievement of Sternberg. (By 1924 the antipathy to Germanic names and titles, so rife during and immediately after the war years in the United States [as Stroheim found out], had abated. Quite incidentally, there *is* an ancient noble family of von Sternbergs in Vienna.)

The *Wanderjahre* continued and now included Paris, Prague, Naples, Berlin, with intermittent forays of film work in London, Hollywood, and New York. On one such he was assistant to William Neill, in 1924, at the F.B.O. studios on Neill's production of *Vanity's Price*, starring Anna Q. Nilsson, adapted from a best-selling novel of the day, *Black Oxen*, by Gertrude Atherton, a story of synthetically preserved youth. The vogue of "rejuvenation" was all the rage. (Dr. Serge Voronoff and his grafting of young monkey glands on old people was as popular in the public fancy as any movie star!) The last scene of the film, given to Sternberg to direct after the director became unavailable, took place in the penumbral chiaroscuro of the operating amphitheatre of a hospital during a "rejuvenation" operation on a woman. Medical students are watching the operation under the glare of the surgical lamp from their gallery seats. Sternberg cross-cut the operation with close-ups of their reactions: one showed disgust, another leaned toward his colleague and leered, a third looked faintly amused. Long after this tawdry film was forgotten, this final scene was remembered. And with it came the first recognition of Sternberg as a director.

The idea of cutting away from an action to show reaction was to become a favorite device of directors, but seldom has it been used meaningfully, to *add* to the action or to comment on it. Years later, Sternberg was to repeat the device in the stunning scene of the reaction of the crowd in the Moroccan café at the initial entrance of Amy Jolly (Marlene Dietrich) in her man's formal evening dress . . . top hat, white tie, and tails . . . notably the marvelous mixed reaction of Legionnaire Tom Brown (Gary Cooper), perhaps the most memorable introduction of a new actress in the annals of the screen.*

In 1924, Sternberg was returning from one of his periodic European junkets on a cattle boat from London to New York, from which he was to continue by bus to Hollywood to start work for the F.B.O. (Film Booking Office) studios. It was on this return to Hollywood that he met George K. Arthur, a young British actor who was trying to break into the movies as a comedian and who had some $4800 to invest in a modest production venture he had in mind, something called *Just Plain Buggs*. Sternberg showed Arthur a scenario he himself had written, *The Salvation Hunters*.

The Salvation Hunters marked the debut of Sternberg as a director, as well as George K. Arthur as an actor, though

---

* One is reminded of Franz Farga's description (in *Violins and Violinists*, London, 1940) of a Paganini concert: "The spell ended and the applause began—with a vehemence never before heard in the Imperial ballroom. People shouted and yelled madly. The magician was still standing on the platform, his face unmoved. His mouth twisted into a wry smile and the glittering eyes, wearing a cunning look, seemed to be mocking the crowd of admirers for behaving so foolishly."

Budget—$4800. The project—*The Salvation Hunters*. What would the future hold? The young Sternberg flanked by his two players, George K. Arthur and Georgia Hale. The lonely beginning. (1924)

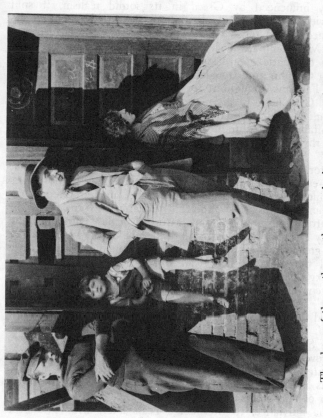

The dregs of the earth . . . the coward, the procurer, and the girl. One of the early scenes of *The Salvation Hunters.* (1924)

not as a comedian. Filmed in and around the mud-flats of San Pedro, south of the Los Angeles dockside wharves, the *leitmotif* was a dredge in San Pedro Bay, scooping up mud into a barge from the bay bottom, which haunted the lives of the film's three characters, a trio of derelicts. Doubtlessly influenced by *Greed* in its sordid realism, it split its viewers into two violently opposed camps—those who loathed it and those who were ecstatic. In the latter camp was Max Reinhardt, who declared, "It is inconceivable that such cinematic greatness could have come from America." Both Chaplin and Douglas Fairbanks also were enthusiastic, and Fairbanks bought it for their company, United Artists. Said Chaplin: "It gives me pleasure to recommend *The Salvation Hunters.* To me it revealed a spontaneous and admirable film technique, combined with artistic composition and rhythm of presentation. It is a great picture—and different." The English pianist, Elly Ney, and the Dutch conductor, Willem van Hoogstraten, said it was the best film they had ever seen. "The handling of the theme is almost symphonic, its simplicity puts it on a plane rarely attained in the motion pictures." "Wonderful!" exclaimed Morris Gest, the theatrical impresario. "I'm wiring Douglas Fairbanks and Mary Pickford tonight that I think *The Salvation Hunters* is the greatest compliment to the American movie public ever paid them by an American director. I was reminded of Gorky's *The Lower Depths* and felt that at last we had a Eugene O'Neill of the screen." It made several of the "Ten Best" lists of 1925. Some time afterwards, Chaplin, being asked to name the best films he had ever seen, replied, "*The Birth of a Nation, Intolerance, Hearts of the World,* and *The Salvation Hunters.*" Chaplin not only took Sternberg's discovery, Georgia Hale, who played the girl in *The Salvation Hunters,* for the feminine lead in *The Gold Rush* but two years later paid him the compliment of entrusting the direction of one of his own productions, *The Sea Gull,* starring Edna Purviance, to Sternberg. Years later, after *The Blue Angel, Morocco, Dishonored,* Sternberg continued to announce himself in the full-page trade ads directors customarily inserted annually in the *Film Daily Year Book:* "Josef von Sternberg—Director of *The Salvation Hunters.*" He never forgot his experiences in the mud-flats of San Pedro and what they meant to him. One does not forget one's first love. (In

Success . . . United Artists, represented here by Douglas Fairbanks, buys *The Salvation Hunters*. George K. Arthur smiles but the dour Sternberg still tries to peer into the future.

the 1950's he designed for himself and his family a luxurious bungalow on the cliffs of the New Jersey palisades overlooking the Hudson River, directly above a dredge like the one in *The Salvation Hunters.*)

Now launched as a full-fledged director, Sternberg was asked by Mary Pickford to guide her in her next picture. It was Ernst Lubitsch who had guided Miss Pickford the year before in *Rosita,* a "Spanish romance" upon which they compromised after she rejected his wish to do *Marguerite and Faust* and he rejected her wish to do *Dorothy Vernon of Haddon Hall.* The result was neither "*echt*-Lubitsch," nor even "*echt*-Pickford," but she determined to try again with another brilliant new "foreign" director. Sternberg's first idea for her had marvelous pictorial possibilities—the world as seen in the imagination of a blind girl who has never seen it. But Miss Pickford did not like the idea of playing a blind girl. So Sternberg left for Pittsburgh to elaborate a story for her against the industrial background of that city. On his return, she asked him to wait before proceeding with the film and Sternberg refused. The project was abandoned. Obviously, the problems of the mechanical age did not interest Miss Pickford, nor did they suit her romantic style. Marshal Neilan replaced Sternberg.

Since MGM had the next option on his services, Sternberg went there to develop Alden Brooks's novel *Escape,* and to write the screenplay with Alice Deuer Miller. Starring Conrad Nagel, Renée Adoree, and Paulette Duval, and titled *The Exquisite Sinner,* the movie was completed in the Spring of 1926. It told the story of a rich young man's running away from a stifling home to live with the gypsies and of his family and fiancée's trying unsuccessfully to induce him to return. The setting is Brittany. It is described by Robert Florey (Sternberg's assistant on the film, and one of the few people who saw it) as "a high comedy almost too subtle for the screen." MGM did not like it and ordered it remade by one Phil Rosen, who managed what Sternberg had done (including his screenplay) beyond recognition. "The result," commented Sternberg years later, "was that they now had two ineffective films instead of one." The remake was called *Heaven on Earth,* today mercifully forgotten.

In the same year, Sternberg began a second film for MGM (under his eight-picture contract), *The Masked Bride,* star-

A contract with MGM follows, the result is *The Exquisite Sinner*—
"too exquisite" for L. B. Mayer, and they remake it. A scene from
the original version. (1925)

Pacific Coast Beach near Santa Monica, on location for *The Exquisite Sinner*. L. to R.—Robert Florey (special French assistant), Max Fabian (cameraman), Nick Grinde (assistant), Paulette Duval (actress), Sternberg, and the ubiquitous musicians to inspire the players with "mood" music, a charming Hollywood fixture of the Twenties.

ring Mae Murray. Florey, who again assisted on the production, says: "He shot only two reels before he became disgusted with his assignment, turned the camera to the ceiling and shot the studio rafters as his departing gesture to the film. But *what* two reels they were! No one saw them except L. B. Mayer and the gang, Sam Winston (Sternberg's cutter), Bill Levanway (MGM's head editor), Sternberg, and myself. Just as in the case of the marvelous first version of *The Exquisite Sinner*, if this one had been finished and kept intact at MGM, it would still be showing today in the ciné-clubs and film societies everywhere; it was a masterpiece. Sternberg never shot a foot of film indifferently. . . ." The contract was broken by mutual consent and the project turned over to Christy Cabanne. Rumors now flew about that the brooding young director with the Oriental mustache and ubiquitous cane was hard to handle and that he objected temperamentally to studio supervision of any kind. At any rate, Sternberg left for a European vacation, to allow Hollywood's attitude toward him to "cool off."

On his return, Chaplin asked him to direct a film intended to bring Chaplin's erstwhile leading lady, Edna Purviance, out of retirement. It was to have been her first serious film since the memorable *A Woman of Paris*, and it was the only occasion when Chaplin entrusted another director with one of his own productions. Titled *The Sea Gull* (no relation to the Chekov play), later titled *A Woman of the Sea*, the film, from an original tale by Sternberg, was a simple love story set against the background of the changing patterns of the sea, which were themselves used for psychological as well as atmospheric underscoring of the action. It was photographed largely on the seacoast of Monterey, California. When it was finished, Chaplin's reaction was that it was too sophisticated for general audiences, that they would not understand it. John Grierson, the eminent Scottish critic, said: "Even a masterful intuition cannot take a man everywhere, and Chaplin has, though I hate to say this, his blind spots. It is my guess, for example, that he is completely blind to the visual beauties of Von Sternberg's *Woman of the Sea*. This picture was made for him and Chaplin failed to release it. I think I know the reason, because I heard Chaplin go over his own version of it two nights before Sternberg showed it to me. Here was Chaplin concentrating on the human drama of the picture—

The second film for MGM is *The Masked Bride*, on a set of which Will Hays (first movie czar), Mae Murray, and Robert Z. Leonard disport themselves as the still dour Sternberg looks on. After several days he quit. *Where was the future?* (1925)

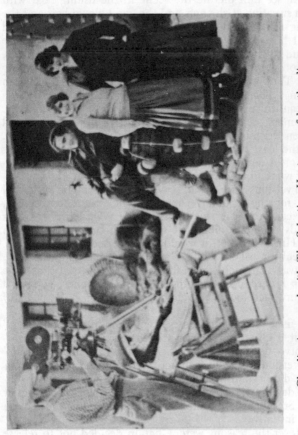

Chaplin, impressed with *The Salvation Hunters*, confides the direction of *The Sea Gull*, from another Sternberg story, to its author in a film designed as a starring vehicle for his loyal leading lady, Edna Purviance (second from right). (1926)

and on nothing else; here was Von Sternberg concentrating on the visual beauty of the picture—and on scarcely anything else! Chaplin's version was magnificent from a humanist point of view: it had feeling in it, emotion, movement: and I can still see him picture the scene in the fishing boat with the men sweating at the nets and the wind-blown hair and the wriggling fish. But beyond that Chaplin was not concerned and is, I believe, never concerned. The visual pattern of the masts and rigging, the pattern of sunlight on the drying nets, the sculpturesque pattern of the human figures were nothing to him. They were everything to Von Sternberg—too much everything! The irony of *Woman of the Sea* is that it is the most beautiful picture ever produced in Hollywood, and the least human. . . . If Chaplin had done it himself it would have been the most human, and, from a visual point of view, one of the least beautiful. There is the issue! Von Sternberg needs a great deal of what Chaplin has: Chaplin needs something of what Von Sternberg has."

"Two versions were made," says Florey. "Chaplin suggested changes for the second version to which Sternberg agreed, without compromising his original idea. The story was over the heads of the audience at the single preview it had in Beverly Hills. However, it would have pleased the movie elite, the 'Boeuf-sur-le-Toit' boys, Cocteau, Picabia, Buñuel, Dali, etc. It was extremely interesting and not as static as *The Salvation Hunters*. The photography was extremely good and Edna Purviance looked much better than in *A Woman of Paris*."

"The final version satisfied neither Chaplin nor Sternberg," commented Grierson. "It was still extraordinarily beautiful—but empty—possibly the most beautiful film I had ever seen." Three versions of the conflict were bruited about: (a) Chaplin didn't understand the film; (b) Eve Sothern outshone Edna Purviance as an actress; (c) Chaplin was upset because Sternberg had arranged the Beverly Hills preview on his own initiative.

Whatever the reasons were, Chaplin decided not to release it. Curiously, Chaplin makes no reference to this film in his autobiography.

Again Sternberg departed for Europe and on his return was approached by Paramount, to be an assistant director again. He accepted. His acceptance was to have notable results, for it led to an association with Paramount that was to last for eight years (1927–1935), during which he did most of his best work, including the discovery of Marlene Dietrich; work that was to make him world famous. When the studio had editing problems with Frank Lloyd's *Children of Divorce*, starring Gary Cooper, Clara Bow, and Einar Hanson, Paramount's production head, B.P. Schulberg, asked Sternberg to look at the picture and make suggestions for recutting. Sternberg saw the footage and declared it didn't just need recutting or even retakes but a completely new story approach. He agreed to do the rewriting, direct the additional scenes, and do the final editing. Half the original footage was discarded and the new half shot by Sternberg in three days of 20-hours-a-day shifts. Since most of the actors were busy on other assignments, he could work with them only when they were free—mostly at night. When the press saw *Children of Divorce* they picked out Sternberg's scenes to comment upon, particularly a sequence showing London's glittering Covent Garden conjured up almost overnight by Sternberg on the studio's back lot. *Children of Divorce* did much to dissipate the myth of Sternberg's intractability. He had salvaged a picture that had been condemned as worthless. The film went on to become a critical and box-office success. He had proved himself a director who could work swiftly and effectively and Schulberg now considered him for a major film, *Underworld*, from a screen original by Ben Hecht about Chicago gangsters and the quasi-Nietzschean world they inhabited. Erich Pommer, then also at Paramount, says that producers then under contract to Paramount were asked by Schulberg to give their opinions of Sternberg's qualifications for this assignment. Unanimously they recommended him for the job.

Early in 1927 Sternberg embarked on the filming of *Underworld* from a scenario written by himself, based on Hecht's 18-page story, which Hecht says he wrote in the form of a film-treatment with Arthur Rosson. Wrote Hecht in his autobiography, *A Child of the Century*: "I made up a movie about a Chicago gunman and his moll, called Feathers McCoy. As a newspaperman I had learned that nice people—the audience—loved criminals, doted on reading about their love problems as well as their sadism. My movie, grounded on this simple truth, was produced with the title, *Under-*

The future has arrived, in just one year . . . *Underworld*, with its swift, laconic style. The pattern for the gangster film is set. George Bancroft, Clive Brook, Evelyn Brent. (1927)

Just as Stroheim had rescued Zasu Pitts from slapstick comedies for *Greed*, Sternberg gave the genial Larry Semon his one chance in a straight role in *Underworld*. Here he is with Evelyn Brent at a gangster's ball.

world. It was the first gangster movie to bedazzle the movie fans and there were no lies in it—except for a half-dozen sentimental touches introduced by its director, Jo von Sternberg." Sternberg admits Hecht was not pleased with the picture and asked that his name be taken off the screen. Yet when the first Academy Awards presentations were made for 1927–28, it was Ben Hecht who won the writing "Oscar" for the "Best Original Screen Story." The film went on to become an enormous box-office success, for which Paramount gave Sternberg a $10,000 bonus. For the first time in film history, a theatre (the big new Paramount palace in New York) had to give midnight showings to accommodate the crowds. *Underworld* was a potent mixture of realism and poetry done in the vernacular of the period, and was to set the pattern for the whole cycle of American gangster films to come, though Fritz Lang may have anticipated this *genre* in his *Dr. Mabuse der Spieler* in 1922, with gangsters firing from escaping automobiles, and so on. At any rate, the *genre* it so eloquently established started a vogue that lasted an entire generation until the outbreak of the Second World War when gangsterism on a much bigger scale made the little criminals of *Underworld* seem petty indeed. But for the cinema, *Underworld* was a milestone in its progress toward maturity. Years later René Clair said in "Reflections on the Cinema" (London, 1953): "When the producers imposed on Sternberg the 'news-item' plot of *Underworld*, or on Feyder the *feuilleton* yarn of *Thérèse Raquin*, they did not suspect that these poor stories would give birth to the poignant screen tragedies we know."

Now the pet of Paramount, Sternberg undertook to fulfill a promise made to Erich von Stroheim to re-edit the latter's *The Wedding March*, which Paramount was releasing and which had been taken away from its director when his own edited version ran to what they regarded as an impossible length. Here, in Sternberg's own words, is what happened: "As I recall, both of us, von Stroheim and I, were under contract to Paramount, though he had finished *The Wedding March* and edited it long before I was assigned to cut it down to releasable length. We were friendly, he had repeatedly expressed admiration for my work. The company had told him to cut it down so that it could be released, and he said he could not. Thereupon it was suggested that others handle it, and, until my name was mentioned, he objected strenuously. He, himself, showed me the film (to my recollection it included everything he intended to show). He asked me personally to take over the assignment, and I did so without any protest on his part. I told him precisely what I would shorten; we were friendly before, during, and afterwards. . . . I showed him the shortened version and he thanked me. Had he objected to anything, I would not only have restored the film to its original length but would have refused to have anything more to do with it. I am explicit about this for it seems to be generally thought that I edited his work without his O.K., which is something I would not have done under any circumstances. . . . I had been strongly impressed with his earlier *Greed* . . . I know nothing about the division of the film into two parts. I never saw the film again and how it was finally shown is unknown to me."

Sternberg next turned to the writing of an original story for Emil Jannings, who, after his international successes in *The Last Laugh*, *Tartuffe*, *Faust*, and *Variety* (especially the latter, which Paramount released in the United States), was brought to Hollywood, where he made his debut in the maudlin *The Way of All Flesh*, a misbegotten attempt to combine his roles as the old porter in *The Last Laugh* with the virile robustness of his trapeze artist in *Variety*. Sternberg's story, *The Street of Sin*, was a Salvation Army tale set in the slums of London's Soho, and featured Fay Wray and Olga Baclanova. Jannings was cast as a Soho bully in it and the direction was turned over to Mauritz Stiller, who had recently arrived from Sweden as the mentor of Greta Garbo, and who was out of a job after he and MGM broke up during the filming of her second American film, *The Temptress*.

The genesis of Sternberg's next directorial effort for Paramount was an anecdote casually told him by Lubitsch (who was also working at Paramount). It was the true story of an ex-Czarist general who, after the Revolution, drifted to Hollywood, like so many others, and found himself playing his own life role on a movie set. Contrary to the screen credits of the film, says Sternberg, Lajos Biro, John S. Goodrich, and Herman J. Mankiewicz had nothing to do with the story treatment or final screenplay of *The Last Command*. Characteristically, it was written by the director himself. The film gave Sternberg an opportunity to castigate the superficiality

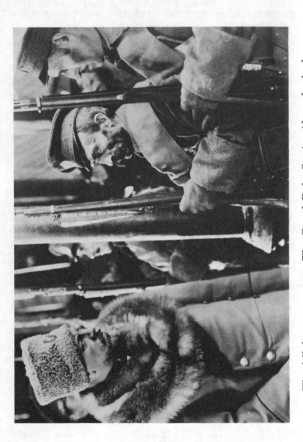

The fall from power . . . The Grand Duke Sergius Alexander lords it over the Russian troops at the front. Emil Jannings in *The Last Command*, that bitter and ironic paragraph from World War I. (1928)

of Hollywood movie making, while initiating what was to become for him a favorite theme, the fall from power of a once formidable being. With the camera flexibility of G. W. Pabst's *Jeanne Ney*, *The Last Command* was a story within a story, told in flashback, exploiting the milieu of Hollywood itself, and great care was taken to separate the two layers of consciousness. It also provided Emil Jannings with his best American role as the proud Russian general who falls from power and grace through circumstances beyond his control.

The critical reception of *The Last Command* was delirious, each reviewer seemed to vie with the others in finding superlatives that would do ample justice to the film's dramatic power. Clearly Sternberg had captivated the popular imagination more completely and overwhelmingly than ever before. Among the first to congratulate him was Douglas Fairbanks: "A psychoanalyst would probably say that my deep enjoyment of *The Last Command* had its foundation in selfishness. And I can't deny that it was soul-warming to have the faith I've always had in you so beautifully justified—feeling, as I do, that I am, in a sense, your *pater in industria*. Can't tell you how fine I think the picture is with its movement, power, and depth of feeling. I know nothing finer in art or literature. Sincerest congratulations!" From Feodor Chaliapin came a telegram: "Saw *Last Command* yesterday. Have rarely experienced such artistic pleasure. Cannot refrain from congratulating you on your admirable work in this splendid production." "The Russian Revolution was not altogether in vain," said the London *Sunday Graphic*, "It has produced *The Last Command*, one of the greatest pictures ever screened." "It is the greatest film in the world. There is no qualifying sentence to that praise of *The Last Command*," wrote the London *Daily Sketch*. The Paramount Office in Berlin received the following wire from Warsaw: "The première of *The Last Command* was sold out to capacity. Screening attended by ministers and members of diplomatic corps. Jannings's work claimed to be better than anything seen before. For the first time in the history of Warsaw, speculators were selling tickets in front of the theatre at higher prices than box office. Many hundreds of people turned away because of lack of seats." In *Theatre Arts* magazine, New York, the "certain, structural touch of Sternberg" was analyzed. "Movement under his hand is not unrelated and

A refugee reduced to playing his former role in a film studio, with its lacerating comments on Hollywood superficialities. The fall from grace was to become a favorite theme of Sternberg. (Emil Jannings in *The Last Command*.)

haphazard, but is built up, tier upon tier, until the peak is attained in some dramatic climax. . . . And once again, as in *Underworld*, Sternberg shows himself a master of suggestion, which implies a willingness to concede the presence of constructive intelligence in his audience." So knowing a director as the late Preston Sturges called *The Last Command* perhaps the only perfect picture he had ever seen.

His favorite "femme fatale" of the period, Evelyn Brent (who was in both *Underworld* and *The Last Command*), was to serve again as the "fatal woman" of Sternberg's next film, *The Dragnet*, another gangster film. For the second time, Sternberg inserted a ballroom scene frenetic with flying confetti and paper streamers (previously seen in *Underworld*), which was to become a favorite pictorial element with him, subsequently demonstrated in *Dishonored* and *The Devil Is a Woman*.

That same year, 1928, Sternberg turned out the pictorially remarkable *Docks of New York*, which earned the praise of George Bernard Shaw. In it George Bancroft (who had become a favorite actor of Sternberg since *Underworld*, appearing in four of his films) moved with the grace of a ballet dancer, despite his heavy bulk, so integrated were his movements. Out of an imagination and sense of fantasy as vivid and evocative as Thomas Burke's evocations of London's Soho and Whitechapel in *Limehouse Nights* (and in an instinctive echo of the ancient Greeks who ordained that "every man owes five days a year to Dionysus"?), Sternberg conjured up a section of the Hoboken waterfront in the studio, complete with a dirty tramp steamer tied up to the dock, its smoke-filled saloons with their wooden staircases outside leading to the upstairs rooms of the cheap prostitutes, the steaming boiler-room in the ship's hold with the glistening bodies of the stokers manning the fire-ovens, the sweating faces of those laboring in front of red-hot coal and looking forward to shore leave, which meant cold beer and the soft, yielding arms of the saloon girls . . . all rendered in photography of the richest chiaroscuro. Except for a fleeting glimpse of the New York skyline and oil slicks on the lapping waters of the bay, *The Docks of New York* was wholly studio-made. The director felt that only on the studio stages could he control the infinite shades of black-and-white photography, which he had developed by this time to an art in

The juxtaposition of serpentine and confetti with characters who live dangerously has become a "high tessitura" of Sternberg's style. (See *Underworld, Dishonored, The Devil Is a Woman*.) William Powell and Evelyn Brent in *The Dragnet*. (1928)

itself. With some of the scenes veiled in artificial mist or harbor fog, the pictorial composition had a dreamlike quality that could not have been obtained in a natural setting under the conditions imposed by the director. (The case of Tissé successfully photographing the harbor fog of Odessa for *Potemkin* was something else—it just happened, and Eisenstein said, "Shoot it!" It was a chance thing, like Eisenstein's chance coming upon the steps of Odessa and suddenly deciding to stage his massacre scene on them. Poetic license takes many forms.) "Half Hogarth, half Mack Sennett," wrote Thomas Quinn Curtiss of it in the Paris *Tribune* many years afterwards, after a showing at the Cinémathèque Française. "A film of pictorial brilliance, telling atmosphere, and some wonderful low humor." He compares it with another waterfront screen drama, *On the Waterfront*, Elia Kazan's film with Marlon Brando, and finds the latter dismally lacking in any unity or conviction in comparison. "From the humanistic standpoint," Curtiss wrote, "the performances are so incredibly good that players and characters seem one." The London *Daily Telegraph* went on to say, "It conveys, quite unobtrusively, a great moral lesson. By a hundred deft touches, Sternberg makes us poignantly aware of some vague, inarticulate longings for something better that may haunt human souls seemingly depraved beyond redemption." As for its technique, a critic of the time wrote: "Let us not forget that the silent film is actually being stifled by its own perfection. Carl Dreyer's *La Passion de Jeanne d'Arc* and Sternberg's *Docks of New York* prove this indubitably. What remains to be done? Repeat the technical triumphs, the wonderful lighting, the overwhelming settings, with actors denuded of staginess as were those who took part in it? No, we have demonstrably reached the culmination of one form of cinematic expression and if the sound film had not been invented, producers the world over would have been looking for something else. . . ."

The Dies Irae of the silent film was already tolling fitfully though its full clangor was not to drown out all else for another year. Made in the transition period from silence to sound, *The Case of Lena Smith*, like some other notable "last minute" silent films of the period, was obscured in the furore attendant upon the debut of the first sound films. It was Sternberg's first film with a Viennese setting, this time

"His world was a battlefield of light and dark," said Goethe of Beethoven. The stoke-hold of a tramp steamer. Clyde Cook and George Bancroft in *The Docks of New York*. (1928)

Sternberg with megaphone, directing a scene from *The Docks of New York*, that ciné-flower plucked from the grime of the lower depths. "The finest film I've ever seen," said Bernard Shaw. (1928)

Dante consigned carnal sinners only to the second circle of hell of
the nine. Sternberg isn't even sure they belong to the first. Betty
Compson was extraordinarily touching in *The Docks of New York*.
Above all, Sternberg was a director of women. (George Bancroft as
the stevedore on a spree.) (1928)

the *fin du siècle* Vienna (1894–1914), the severe caste-ridden citadel of anti-Semitism and reaction in Europe, which despite its intoxication with Lehar's *The Merry Widow* and its great annual Spring Flower Parade of the "upper ten thousand" rolling in their fancy carriages through the Prater, was termed by one of its most distinguished citizens, Sigmund Freud, "disgusting in the highest degree." So much for "alt Wien," gay old Vienna and the already rotting Hapsburg dynasty and its glittering panoply during its long, protracted sunset. Fair it may have been to see from the outside (as Winston Churchill remarked, looking back, in his *The World Crisis*), but all its culture could not save it from the Junkerism that held it in thrall until the incident at Sarajevo and that fatal day in August, 1914 when the guns "gloriously" boomed. Against this bittersweet background, Sternberg told the pitiful story of a peasant girl who secretly marries a profligate army officer, bears him a child, and becomes a servant in his father's house. When the father attempts to take her child, she rails against him as a tyrant. The callousness and prejudice of the officer class was limned with unrelenting harshness, but with incisive psychological insight, too, for the weak but well-meaning seducer of the girl, helpless to help her when her child is placed in an orphanage by his father, shoots himself. And the desperate terror of Lena's flight from the orphanage with her child— dirty, torn, and bloody, a fugitive from the law, making her way back to her village in the country—is one of the great searing passages in the cinema. "Lena's flight," wrote Dwight Macdonald in the March, 1931, *Miscellany,* "is expressed by the camera following her like a watchful eye as she moves along a wall, hiding behind water pipes and shrinking into dark corners. . . . Von Sternberg does not use his skill in handling the camera to avoid coming to grips with his story. His attack is direct, aggressive, bringing out all the power of his theme, the love, nay, urge, of a mother for her child. . . . 'Note that most good films are characterized by very simple themes and relatively uncomplicated action,' is a remark by Pudovkin that applies well to *The Case of Lena Smith. . . .* I regard it as the most completely satisfying American film I have seen."

It was Sternberg's last silent film.

How would he make the transition to the sound film? Let

Finally Sternberg evokes the "Old Vienna" of his youth, but the rake-hell lieutenant-seducer and the pretty servant girl are no longer stock characters but creatures who suffer under Junker tyranny. His last silent film, *The Case of Lena Smith*. (1928—what a year for him!)

"*Wien, Wien, nur du allein . . . !*" Vienna, Vienna, only you . . . !
The paroxysmic escape of the young mother from a reformatory, in
search of her child. Dwight Macdonald has written lyrically of this
sequence. Esther Ralston in *The Case of Lena Smith*. (1928)

a telegram to Sternberg from the German director of A *Waltz Dream* fame, Ludwig Berger, one of the shining lights of Ufa, then also in Hollywood, answer: "I saw your film *Thunderbolt* and congratulate you with my heart. It is the first fully realized and artistically accomplished sound film . . . Bravo!" *Thunderbolt* was a return by Sternberg to the milieu of the gangster film that he had made so uniquely his own. This time he told a prison story that was startling even for him in its brutality of theme and its all but unbearable suspense in the film's second half; it is set in the death house of a federal penitentiary where the merciless account of crime, revenge, and punishment grinds to a terrible halt when the gangster boss, "Thunderbolt," is led to the electric chair. There was no background music. The photography was cold and gray. It was a work of realism, unprettified in the slightest degree. *The Salvation Hunters* had been such a work. But *The Salvation Hunters* ended on a note of hope. *Thunderbolt* ends hopelessly. Had success made of the artist a pessimist? End of the first phase . . .

The advent of the sound film and the resultant return to Germany from Hollywood of Emil Jannings (because of his bad English) and Erich Pommer (ordered to return by Ufa, to which he was still under contract) was to mark a turning point in Sternberg's career. Among Pommer's first tasks, as production head of Ufa, was to launch Jannings's return to the German screen in 1929 in the latter's first talking film.

Sternberg was sent for at the request of Jannings and on his arrival in Berlin was shown by Jannings a novel, *Professor Unrat*, a violent attack on Imperial Germany, written in 1905 by Heinrich Mann (brother of Thomas Mann), who had remained on the political left after the 1918 revolution. The book was a dissimulated attack on bureaucracy, symbolized by Professor Rat,* a model of bourgeois virtue and discipline with "feet of clay," who succumbs to the tempta-

---

* In German the name "Rat" has the connotation of "counsellor" but the Professor's students nickname him "unrat"—"unclean" (or even *merde*)—a classification for the stuffy bureaucrat, also. (Originally, G.W. Pabst had planned to film *Professor Unrat* but this didn't materialize. Jannings' first suggestion to Sternberg was a film on Rasputin, which Sternberg rejected.)

With his first sound film, Sternberg returns again to the *milieu* of *Underworld* and the gangster prototype set by George Bancroft. There was no background music, only source music, another innovation that was to become characteristic of him. *Thunderbolt*. (1929)

tions of a sluttish cabaret singer, for all his middle-class façade of respectability, and then goes on to become an important social figure. Pommer and Sternberg agreed that here were the possibilities for a strong human characterization by Jannings but the story itself would have to be rewritten. In the adaptation by Sternberg, the Professor Rat of the film is not the character in the book—Sternberg created a new character, a new "psychology," that was appropriate to the art of the film. What was good as literature would be lost in a literal interpretation and transposition to the screen. The last third of the novel was dispensed with altogether. Sternberg says that Robert Liebmann helped him with the German dialogue. Pommer says Carl Zuckmayer contributed some details. Karl Vollmoeller, who had previously accompanied Sternberg on a world tour, did some minor revisions on the script at Sternberg's request. Sternberg says he directed the picture from his own notes; there wasn't any "screenplay." Henry F. Pringle in his "Profile" of Sternberg in *The New Yorker* magazine of March 28, 1931, affirmed: "He interferes with his writers so much that scenarists avoid working with him when they can." Many things in the film were inserted by Sternberg that are not to be found in the book, such as the leitmotif of the apostle-clock admonishing the listener to practice "virtue and sincerity until the grave," the Professor's pet bird (to illustrate his loneliness), the silent clown who presages the Professor's becoming a clown himself, the wedding celebration, the jilted Professor, now a clown, imitating a rooster, the Professor's frenzied insanity when he sees Lola with her new lover, and his dazed return to his old classroom where he embraces his desk (symbol of his former dignity) in the grip of death. Characteristic of Sternberg was his reply to an interpretation by film students giving the Professor's loss of mind as being due to his humiliation rather than to his infatuation with Lola-Lola. "The loss of his mind was an invention of mine. It was to show his incapacity to deal with reality. I would not wish to defend this, as the pathology of insanity is not easily traced, nor does it necessarily follow an indulgence in foolish behavior. Insanity is due to many causes over which the victim has little control and it has afflicted many great men whose lives were exemplary. The study of insanity belongs to the specialist in psychiatry and not to the student of motion pictures."

Pommer wanted Lucie Mannheim for the role of the siren, Lola-Lola, and Jannings agreed, but Sternberg refused to accept the unglamorous Miss Mannheim for a picture that was costing Ufa a half-million dollars, for Germany a very high budget at that time. Heinrich Mann suggested his girl friend, the actress Trude Hesterberg, while Sternberg, meanwhile, was trying to sign Brigitte Helm, who wasn't available.

By chance, Sternberg saw Marlene Dietrich in a play, *Zwei Kravatten*, by Georg Kaiser, where he was supposed to watch Hans Albers, who had been suggested for the minor role of Mazeppa, the circus artist who steals Lola away from the Professor.

From the moment Sternberg noticed Dietrich on the stage he knew he had found his Lola, but neither she nor the heads of Ufa were sure she could do it. It took a lot of persuasion before she agreed to a screen test. Sternberg was pleased with it and Pommer, who always protected the artistic choice of his directors, approved the signing of Miss Dietrich.

Since the accent of the story was now changed from the Professor to Lola-Lola, the title of the film was changed from *Professor Unrat* to *The Blue Angel*, the name of the cabaret where she sang. Heinrich Mann realized that his literary contribution to the future success of this film would be insignificant compared to Sternberg's vision. Sternberg made it clear that the film would not be based on but only stimulated by the novel. When the film was finished, Jannings asked Mann what he thought of his performance, to which the author replied brusquely, "The success of the film will rely in a great measure on the naked thighs of Miss Dietrich!"

Alfred Hugenberg, the industrialist head of Ufa and an old Junker, found a disconcerting resemblance, physically, between himself and the jilted Professor Rat portrayed by Jannings. He also objected to any association of Heinrich Mann with the film, since the novel had been written to discredit Prussian authority, and he refused to endorse the release of the film for its première scheduled for April 1, 1930, at Ufa's flagship theatre, the Palast am Zoo. Sternberg had already left for the United States, without waiting for the opening. Pommer, desperate, asked Mann for a statement confirming that the meaning of his novel had been reversed in the film. Mann's reply was: "Had I been more mature

And then it happened—the epochal discovery of Marlene Dietrich for the Lola-Lola role in *The Blue Angel*. "Not your acting," said Heinrich Mann to its star, Jannings, "will determine the success of this film but her thighs!" The most celebrated of all German sound films. (1930)

"The shot heard 'round the world"—the most famous of all Sternberg scenes—Dietrich about to sing "Ich bin von Kopf bis Fuss auf
Liebe eingestellt" ("Falling in love again") in *The Blue Angel*.

(when I wrote it), I would have developed the character of Professor Unrat more humanly, as in the film."

But Hugenberg was not appeased by Mann's implied withdrawal from the authorship of *The Blue Angel*. Already under the spell of the growing Nazi movement, Hugenberg adamantly refused to allow the film to open, inspiring one of the reactionary Berlin newspapers to publish an attack on Heinrich Mann and his whole literary output. This was answered by an article by Pommer in the *Berliner Tageblatt* stating that Ufa was proud of the film. The struggle within the hierarchy of Ufa went on till the very eve of the première when Hugenberg, to protect his investment, finally relented. Instinctively, Hugenberg, the real power behind the forces of German reaction, had sensed that, within the framework of an entertainment film, Sternberg had subtly mirrored the paranoiac tendencies of the Prussian bourgeoisie. But Sternberg has denied any political intent. "I went to Germany to make *The Blue Angel* without any knowledge of the conditions there—mine was an artist's pilgrimage, and no more. I would like to caution against the reading of too much into it unless the film itself clearly articulates its meaning. I am not partial to mystification."

The première of *The Blue Angel* was, of course, a great success * but Dietrich left Berlin that same night for Bremerhaven to depart for America. At Sternberg's recommendation, Paramount had offered her a contract and she accepted. She followed her director to Hollywood,† where he was already engaged in looking for a story for her next film, which was, in fact, to introduce her to American audiences, even before the release of *The Blue Angel* in the United States by Paramount, which had already acquired the rights. (So real were the scenes in the film that the eminent violinist, Josef Szigeti, in his autobiography, *With Strings Attached*, compared a café-cabaret he had visited in Hamburg during a tour to the sleazy joint in *The Blue Angel*.)

Back in California in the San Fernando valley, in a steel house designed by himself like a small castle, complete with

---

* Some time later, James Joyce told Dietrich that he had seen her in *The Blue Angel*, to which she replied, "Then, monsieur, you have seen the best of me."

† I met her at the pier in New York.

a moat surrounding it,* Sternberg housed a magnificent collection of modern art, one of the most notable private collections in the United States. He was himself a not untalented painter and sculptor, as attested by some landscapes, some incisive portraits, and a virile bronze torso. He also became the subject of sculptures by Rudolf Belling, David Edstrom, and Peter Balbusch and of paintings by Boris Deutsch and David Siqueiros.

It was Dietrich who suggested to Sternberg an obscure novel, *Amy Jolly* (subtitled *The Woman of Marrakech*), by Benno Vigny, which was to serve as the inspiration for their first American film together, *Morocco*,† in which she received second billing to Gary Cooper, just as in Berlin she received second billing to Jannings in *The Blue Angel*. After those two films she received star billing. She had scored a personal triumph unmatched by any actress on the screen since the florescence of Garbo. (Incidentally, the two have never met, although Dietrich always wanted to. What a confrontation of *monstres sacrés* that would be!).

"I have nothing to learn from Europe," Sternberg had said before departing for Germany and *The Blue Angel*. ‡ On his return to Hollywood he proved it by developing and elaborating his own highly personal style, which was to become increasingly more baroque, obsessed as he became with the succession of films he was forced by Paramount and Dietrich to make for her after *Morocco*, a kind of theme and variations on the subject of the love goddess, the twentieth-century Venus in the new mythology of the screen. The screen Dietrich was solely Sternberg's invention, though rooted in an old image of the movies, the mysterious *femme fatale*.

* The moat was very characteristic of Von Sternberg, for even those who thought they were closest to him felt an intellectual "moat" around him that was impossible to cross unless he "let the drawbridge down." The inscrutable Buddhalike mask of his visage was always a formidable warning of this.

† One has only to read the novel *Amy Jolly* to see how different and how much better the film is. Again, as in the case of *Professor Unrat* vs. *The Blue Angel*, the film version amounted to a completely original work. In both cases, the original acted only as a "stimulus" (Sternberg's word) for the new work.

‡ So much has been written about *The Blue Angel* that its stunning world success needs no detailing here.

Here was the old Greek legend (that had served Shaw so well) of Pygmalion and Galatea being enacted all over again, between the artist and his creation, and even the story of Svengali and Trilby, if you will, though when an interviewer for the London *Daily Sketch* in 1936 asked Dietrich if she felt Sternberg had been her Svengali, she replied with a mischievous smile, savoring the words deliciously, "I only wish he had been!"

Morocco premièred December 6, 1930. From Sergei Eisenstein (then in Hollywood) came a telegram: "Of all your great works, *Morocco* is the most beautiful. Admiration and love to you and Marlene." Robert E. Sherwood, then a film critic but soon to become one of America's most distinguished playwrights, said: "*Morocco* should come as a message of reassurance for those who have lately been depressed by the justifiable conviction that imagination is dead in Hollywood. It is a real film, taking advantage of the extraordinary opportunities for dramatic expression that the camera affords, making full and appropriate usage of sound, and placing a negligible emphasis on spoken words." Then he goes on to describe the wonderful scene of the dinner party celebration of the engagement of LeBessière and Amy Jolly, when the conversation falters as the distant drums and bugles of the returning Legionnaires are heard. "There is hardly a single scene in *Morocco* which is not equally artful in its capitalization of the advantages of sound. It never is allowed to interfere with the film's essential pictorial qualities, but it amplifies and enriches them to an incalculable extent. One must congratulate Josef von Sternberg on the best job of direction—of imaginative conception—that has been performed since the screen found its voice. It is incredible to me that anyone can see the results he has achieved in *Morocco* and still say that the old spell of the movies has been broken."

Georgia Hale, in a letter to Sternberg, quotes Chaplin as saying after attending the première with her, "Yes, he is an artist . . . it's his best film." Chaplin felt he took something away with him after seeing it, she said, because it was so beautiful.

Morocco was done with a supple sense of rhythmic phrase. The rhythm is never four-square; the action flows through, to use a musical equivalent, the bar-line from scene to scene.

It is the ultimate meaning of each scene, not the bar-lines, that condition this cinematographic flow and it is a lesson in cinema metrics. Sternberg, here, effaced the last vestiges of demarcation between the silent and the sound film and even the dialogue seems almost incidental in its reticence.

(In *Morocco* also appears the first of the black cats that are to silently stalk through subsequent Sternberg films, as in *Dishonored* and *Macao*.)

Chaplin had ridiculed the coming of sound in the opening scene of *City Lights* and resisted it longer than anyone else; René Clair was desolate over it and said it marked the end of the cinema's florescence—then went on to make three brilliant sound films in a row, *Sous les Toits de Paris*, *Le Million*, *À Nous la Liberté*; in the U.S.S.R., Eisenstein, Pudovkin, and Alexandrov heralded it as the dawn of a new era and issued their famous manifesto on the sound film—which, alas, was never to be realized. Sternberg welcomed sound heartily. Demanding and getting control over every aspect of his films, he was no longer at the mercy of movie house pianists or organists for the music. Now he could control even that by putting such music as he wished on the sound track of the films themselves. The strange thing is that he really, at least in the beginning, did not wish any "background music" for his films. There is not a note of such "atmospheric" music in *Thunderbolt*, *The Blue Angel*, *Morocco*, and *Dishonored*— what music is in them comes from natural sources as integral parts of the action. It takes assurance and courage to do that; few directors then or even now would risk it. Most of the time, music is used as a kind of dubious crutch on which the director leans, hoping the "surge" of the music will "fill in" and make up for any deficiencies his films might otherwise have. However, when background music is used properly, to heighten the intensity (or contrapuntally, though this use is very rarely found), it can be very effective, as music is a legitimate corollary to film and, indeed, in the silent days all films were shown with musical accompaniment. The background music Sternberg used for *The Scarlet Empress* was a notable example of how effective this device can be when controlled by a master, as in the last scene, the triumph of Catherine as Empress against the pealing bells and cannonade of the closing peroration of Tchaikovsky's thunderous *1812 Overture*, with the smiling and breathless Catherine in the

white uniform of a hussar standing by her magnificent white
stallion (almost as handsome as she was) and doves, harbinger
of a new era of peace for Holy Russia, fluttering about her
. . . Pabst told me it was for him one of the peaks of cinema
achievement. Another instance of Sternberg's felicitous use
of background music was the surprise entrance of Don
Pasquale during the carnival ball at the rendezvous of Don
Antonio and Concha in their box in *The Devil Is a Woman*.
The double doors swing open to the passionate Spanish
chant of *Venga Jaleo*, with its flamenco wail, already old
when the Moors were in Andalusia, and there stands the
jealous Don Pasquale against a huge mural of a *corrida*—the
matador about to close in for the kill. . . .

Morocco, like *The Blue Angel*, swept the world. When
Sternberg found himself in Cannes some time afterwards,
he met the Pasha of Marrakech who asked him why he had
not visited him while in his domain. "I told him," says
Sternberg in his autobiography, "I would have paid my
respects had I ever been in Morocco, whereupon he said he
had seen a film of mine and that it contained scenes photographed on streets that he recognized. He smiled when I told
him that this was no more than an accidental resemblance,
a flaw due to my lack of talent to avoid such similarity."
"Two Orientals" jousting with each other. Saladin couldn't
have said it better. It is one of Sternberg's favorite anecdotes
because it reinforces his belief that it is not necessary to go
to the actual locales to achieve realism if you understand
the essence of the reality you're after. An edge of the Sahara
Desert was recreated on the Paramount studio's back lot for
Morocco, just as years later he was to reconstruct a South
Pacific jungle island in a Japanese studio for *Anatahan*.*

Hardly had Sternberg said that he now wanted to go his

* What the layman or average observer fails to comprehend is
that the creative process makes its own demands and that the greatest of these demands is upon the work itself. Joyce Cary, that modern renaissance man of arts and letters, said that audiences had an
obligation to educate themselves so that they could comprehend
the artist's form of communication. On the relationship of art and
fact, he said: "Only art can convey both the fact and the feeling
about the fact, for it works in the medium of common sympathies,
common feeling, universal reaction to color, sound, form. It is the
bridge between souls, meaning by that not only men's minds but
their character and feeling."

separate way when he found himself working on a third picture with Dietrich. This time he devised a story for her loosely based on the exploits of a notorious World War I woman spy working for the Central Powers. The setting was again the harsh pre-World War I Vienna of *The Case of Lena Smith*, a somber film, fitfully lit with a kind of desperate gaiety, flecked with glints of sardonic dialogue, darkly whirling around its black theme of death in war with something of love and decency straining hopelessly to survive the senseless carnage—the whole made fluid and malleable in the creative imagination of the artist. *Dishonored* is to the cinema what Ravel's *La Valse* is to music—the Viennese waltz disintegrating into the First World War.

Sternberg next turned to *An American Tragedy*, from the novel by Theodore Dreiser, which Paramount wished him to make after they rejected Eisenstein's scenario on the same story. Although Sternberg and Eisenstein were friends (Sternberg was the only one in Hollywood who signed an affidavit permitting Eisenstein's re-entry into the United States on the latter's way back from Mexico to the U.S.S.R. after Eisenstein's abortive Mexican film venture), Sternberg never saw Eisenstein's script nor did he ever discuss it with him. (Eisenstein was already in Mexico when Sternberg began work on the film.) Although Samuel Hoffenstein was credited for the scenario, Sternberg says Hoffenstein collaborated with him only on the treatment and that the final scenario was by himself (Sternberg). The dialogue used was Dreiser's own. Every bit of conversation in the film came directly from the novel. But Dreiser felt the film had betrayed his book, which indicted society for Clyde Griffiths's murder of his inamorata so he could marry a rich girl. Dreiser claimed that Clyde Griffiths's sense of values was corrupted by society and his religious background (his parents were missionaries) and that the social implications of his novel were bypassed by the film. He sued Paramount and lost. Two of the foremost critics of the time defended Sternberg's film. Pare Lorentz said: "It is an important picture, not because of the novel but in spite of it." And Benjamin De Casseres said, "It is far superior to the book, which is tripe. The film has raised this tripe to the dignity of good hokum." Although the film was not a popular success in the United States, it was a big success in Europe.

By this time, Sternberg was one of the few American directors whose name appeared on theatre marquees along with the stars, both in the United States and abroad, and sometimes even without the stars.

Vanity Fair, then America's most distinguished magazine of the arts, placed him on a par with Eisenstein (issue of January, 1932) and the brilliant Berlin monthly, *Der Querschnitt*, that same year ran a symposium on "American Titans" in which he was included along with Sinclair Lewis, Andrew Mellon, and Theodore Dreiser.

Dietrich recalls that "In those days of block-booking, Paramount would offer exhibitors 'two Marlene Dietrichs' per year, before we had any idea of what they would be about, but we had to produce them on schedule just the same. More than once we were told in the middle of one picture that we must begin the next immediately after finishing the current one. In those circumstances he [Sternberg] had no choice but to make up his own stories."

And so Dietrich appeared as Shanghai Lily in her next picture with Sternberg, *Shanghai Express*, one of their greatest successes. Just as Sternberg had never been to Morocco before making *Morocco*, he had never been to China before making *Shanghai Express*. He said he was not interested in a "realistic China"—he wanted only to *evoke* China on the screen as an impressionist painter might. It was one of his most characteristic attitudes and was to be carried even further by him in *The Scarlet Empress* and *The Devil Is a Woman*, where he similarly evoked the Byzantine Russia of Catherine the Great and the rococo Spain of Pierre Louys in a style of "high cinema baroque" unprecedented up to that time and, indeed, never repeated by him or anyone else since. Following a private showing, Mary Pickford wrote Sternberg: "Douglas and I saw *Shanghai Express* at the house the other night and we loved it. I think it's your best picture. . . . Sorry I missed seeing *Dishonored*, as everyone speaks so enthusiastically of it. Am looking forward to catching up with it. Douglas joins me in best wishes and congratulations." And Robert E. Sherwood wrote: "*Shanghai Express* is a technological triumph . . . for the principal protagonist of this drama is a railroad train, a perfect vehicle for the expression of von Sternberg's peculiar intelligence. He has recorded the progress of this vehicle with such remarkable expertness that one is given no opportunity to worry about the insufficiency of its mortal cargo. . . . Indeed, I was sorry to leave the train at its final destination. . . . He knows more than anyone else how to use the marvelous mechanical equipment at his disposal. He can make his camera talk and his microphone listen in a positively human manner. Thus, he establishes communion with the physical senses of his audience and he exploits this communion with remarkable skill. . . . Beautiful shot follows beautiful shot but no matter what Clive Brook is saying to Marlene Dietrich the Shanghai Express is speeding on." Everyone was enthralled, especially, with the color, atmosphere, and plangency of the opening scenes preparatory to the Shanghai Express's leaving for its trip. The late Leslie Howard remarked on this, "There you have a definite feeling of reality conveyed in the movement and sound of the train and of the people on the platform and the crowded village."

Shanghai Express was followed by *Blonde Venus*, a sentimental story in which Dietrich, looking more beautiful in each new film made by Sternberg with her, was now more beautiful than ever. Perhaps it was to make up for a lack of a real story. In any case, it had its share of Sternbergian *bizarrerie*, such as the "Hot Voodoo" number that Dietrich sang in a fantastic blonde "fuzzy-wuzzy" wig after emerging startlingly in all her lissomeness from the hairy ugliness of an ape-skin. Its vivid evocation of the American South was particularly striking, utilizing the full range of black-and-white chiaroscuro with dazzling effect.

In August of 1932 Sternberg received a moving letter from the Mexican painter, Siqueiros: "Once more I ask for your help, but it is your own fault, because you're the only one in Los Angeles that has a conscience about art and who understands the lives of those dedicated to this activity. I am locked in Los Angeles and cannot get out of it for lack of money. I have to be in New York for my exhibition in two weeks and you are the only one who can help me. . . . I want you to buy the painting of the enclosed photograph. I want the money to buy an old car to make the trip to New York with my family and my paintings. Thank you." Needless to add, Sternberg bought the painting.

In November 1932 Sternberg left for the West Indies with his cameraman of *The Sea Gull*, Paul Ivano, to shoot backgrounds for a circus story he planned to do next with Miss Dietrich. He was primarily in search of a hurricane, which obstinately refused to materialize, so he abandoned the project and left for another extended holiday in Europe.

On his return he started work on his next film with Dietrich, *The Scarlet Empress*, episodes in the life of Catherine the Great based on her private diaries. Meanwhile, Paramount believed a change of director for her would be in everyone's interest and suggested that she might like to make *The Song of Songs*, from the Sudermann novel, for Rouben Mamoulian. Von Sternberg advised her to accept. He felt it would be good for her to experience a change in director.

Sternberg evoked for *The Scarlet Empress* a Peterhof Palace such as never was and yet was never anything else but Russian, eighteenth-century Byzantine Russian. The twisted, anguished sculptures of saints and martyrs were gargoyles sprung, like Athena from the head of Zeus, from the unendingly fecund imagination of the director and masterfully executed under his supervision by the Swiss sculptor, Peter Balbusch, a long-time Sternberg devotee. Similarly, Richard Kollorsz, a German painter, executed ikons and portraits more Byzantine than any real ikons of the Russian Orthodox Church. Just as Eisenstein a decade later was to heighten the Kremlin palace of Ivan the Terrible with a poetic realism, Sternberg heightened the Peterhof Palace the same way—and not only the décor but the very characters themselves—but Sternberg did it first. In the same way, the elaborate ritual of the wedding of Catherine and Peter in the Cathedral of Kazan in Sternberg's film antedates the elaborate ritual of the coronation of Ivan IV in the Ouspensky cathedral in Eisenstein's. It was this that caused Henri Langlois, curator of the Cinémathèque Française (and an avowed admirer of Eisenstein), to cable Sternberg, after he had belatedly seen *The Scarlet Empress* in March, 1964: "Have just seen marvelous *Scarlet Empress*. Stop. What grand film. Stop. All *Ivan Grozhny* comes from your film. Stop. All my respect and admiration." After World War II, when Pabst came to America to try to persuade Garbo to play the dual roles of Penelope and Circe in his project to film Homer's *Odyssey*, I discussed Sternberg with him. He confessed that whenever he heard that *The Scarlet Empress* was being shown anywhere in Europe, he would drop whatever he was doing and rush to see it. "I look at the screen," he said in awe, "I don't believe I see what I am seeing, but there it is! I think I am losing my mind, it is so incredible!" It was Pabst's way of saying it was the most eye-smiting film he had ever seen. A popular critic of the period when *The Scarlet Empress* first appeared (her name was Elsie Finn) began her review: "Has Josef von Sternberg gone mad? Has the cinema turned like Frankenstein's monster on the director who came closer to giving it life than most others within its shadow?"

"It is not reality that matters in a film," says Chaplin in his autobiography, "but what the imagination can make of it. . . . When I realize how distorted even recent events have become, history as such only arouses my skepticism—whereas a poetic interpretation achieves a general effect of the period. After all, there are more valid facts and details in works of art than there are in history books." In short, in the creative process, art is often anti-fact and fact anti-art.

Following the release of *The Scarlet Empress* to a "mixed" reception, B.P. Schulberg, production chief of Paramount, left that studio for Columbia. He was succeeded at Paramount by Ernst Lubitsch, who not only agreed to let Sternberg make still another film with Dietrich—the last he was due to direct for the studio under his contract—but also persuaded Dietrich to sign a new long-term contract.

Paramount had long owned the rights to Pierre Louys's novel *Woman and Puppet,* filmed by them in 1920 with Geraldine Farrar as the ruthless Spanish sorceress, Conchita Perez, who seduces, ridicules, and finally destroys a middle-aged officer of the Civil Guard. Sternberg wanted to call his version *Caprice Espagnole* but Lubitsch decided on *The Devil Is a Woman.* It went into production early in 1935, ironically enough at the moment Elisabeth Bergner, Dietrich's idol of her Berlin days, had finished in England Alexander Korda's version of *Catherine the Great.*

During the shooting, Von Sternberg stated that *The Devil Is a Woman* would be his last picture with Dietrich. "Miss Dietrich and I," he said, "have progressed as far as possible together. My being with her any further will not help her or me. If we continued we would get into a pattern which would be harmful to both of us." "As far as possible" resulted in the most bewitchingly beautiful photography (Sternberg took screen credit for the photography of this one himself, although he had always supervised the photography of his films), a now ravishingly beautiful Dietrich as Sternberg's camera witchery caught her, the most fantastically impressionistic sets of a dream Spain, and the most audacious gowns with which the director costumed his star.

Louys's title for *Woman and Puppet* was derived from Goya's *Tapices, XLII*: "In the meadow of Manzanares four young Spanish women toss a male puppet in a blanket." Goya's small painting of this scene is in the Prado. The novel is a study in sado-masochism and a minor masterpiece of its *genre*. (It will be recalled that Louys was Oscar Wilde's favorite French novelist.) Its heroine is the *femme fatale* carried to the *n*th degree: *"Elle se faisait mal non pour le plaisir de pécher mais pour la joie de faire mal à quelqu'un."* (*Vide* Stroheim's heroine in his novel, *Paprika*.) But, as Richard Griffith (ex-curator of the Film Library of the Museum of Modern Art in New York) pointed out, "Such a literal devil could no longer be brought to the American screen intact and the Concha Perez of this film emerged as a coquette." But if she was a coquette, she was that *genre* raised to its ultimate power, also, and the difference for most of her victims was academic. Concha no longer danced naked but sang a risqué song. The end result for her victims was the same.

"This is the masterpiece of Josef von Sternberg," wrote the Uruguayan critic, Emil Rodriguez Monegal, "directed with the greatest freedom. It offers in all its glory the absurd Spain of the foreigner—Spanish music *à la* Rimsky-Korsakov in the background, the German Marlene as an improbable Andalusian enchantress, and Goya and Spanish baroque as seen through the eyes of a German expressionist. Yet it is a film of enormous stylistic persuasion and sophisticated grace. The director has made luminous in this extreme achievement that woman of such presence and seductive sexuality that must have been (and still is?) Marlene Dietrich."

There were other things, too, to smite the eye, like the incredible shot of the snowbound train, unwittingly carrying Concha and the officer she will bedevil. It is all but covered with snow, as if an avalanche had descended upon it and engulfed it. Only the very tops of the train windows are still visible. It is absolutely the *ne plus ultra* of being snowbound—it is, as I said, incredible—and it is magnificent. There is the bewitching opening, of the pre-Lenten carnival and its frenzy of serpentine, with its stunningly beautiful serpent in the person of Concha in her carriage threading her way through the maze of merrymakers and, always and unceasingly, there are those grotesque masks, dwarfs and satyrs darting through the whirling lights and shadows, and a puppet with which the puppet himself (the bedeviled officer) toys. There is even a golliwog jack-in-the-box who delivers a note of assignation from Concha to her newest victim—echoes of all the gargoyles of *The Scarlet Empress*. There is the duel in the rain which is like a shower of diamonds on the glistening participants and Concha, herself, already swathed in black for whichever of her dueling lovers will not emerge from the fray over her. There is, in short, scarcely a moment in this extraordinary work without its own wonder.

Then a curious thing happened. The Republican government of Spain objected officially to the film for its portrayal of an officer of the Civil Guard being made ridiculous by a (shall we say?) loose woman. On October 31, 1935, the Spanish Minister of War, Gil Robles, announced that all Paramount films would be barred in Spain unless *The Devil Is a Woman* was immediately withdrawn from world circulation and the negative burned. A commercial treaty being planned at that time between the United States and Spain was rumored as the reason for the quick capitulation to this arrogant ultimatum, which was little less than blackmail. Entitled "Susceptibilité Excessif," an article in *Intercine*, official film publication of the League of Nations in Rome, commented: *"L'Espagne de von Sternberg n'était et n'a jamais été l'Espagne: c' était un pays imaginaire, un pays de conte, une espèce de paradis artificiel et romantique peuplé des fantasmes carnavalesques et d'amours impossibles. . . . Pourquoi ce féroce autodafé?"* Clearly the Spanish Republican government lacked a sense of humor. It has since been learned that Paramount did *not* burn the negative and that the real reason for the Spanish government's attitude was that a wealthy Spanish industrialist promised to build a complex of modern studios in Madrid if he could be guaranteed a minimum of competition from foreign films. Whatever the reasons, *The Devil Is a Woman* had a limited circulation. It remains the favorite of all the films they did together, of both the director and star. The Dietrich "episode" in the career of Sternberg was over. End of the second phase . . .

Sternberg then rejoined Schulberg at Columbia where he made two films, *Crime and Punishment*, after Dostoievski, and *The King Steps Out*, from the operetta, *Cissy*, by Herbert and Ernst Marischka, with music drawn from Fritz Kreisler. Only a nimble mind could jump from Louys to Dostoievski and then to a Kreisler operetta. The true artist encompasses the whole world. From the Kreisler trifle Sternberg was soon to make another spectacular jump, to the decadent world of the Roman Emperor Claudius. The break with Paramount had freed him from his tie with Dietrich and its countless variations on a single theme. His brief experience at Columbia was not a felicitous one for him, lacking as he did the freedom and the largesse he enjoyed at Paramount.

He decided he needed a respite from films and took off on a leisurely trip around the world. On the return leg of the long journey he became ill and entered a London nursing home. Upon his recovery, Alexander Korda proposed a partnership with him in London Films, which Sternberg rejected, but when Korda then asked him to salvage a project he (Korda) had initiated, the filming of *I, Claudius*, from the historical novel by Robert Graves, Sternberg accepted the directorial reins. The year was now 1936. Korda had been having difficulties with Charles Laughton in the title role, despite the great success these two had with *The Private Life of Henry VIII*. Merle Oberon was to play Messalina and others in the cast were Flora Robson, Robert Newton, and Emlyn Williams.

Sets were designed by Vincent Korda, and Georges Périnal was the cameraman. Having already played Nero in De Mille's *Sign of the Cross* (1933), Laughton was thought to be a "natural" for Tiberius Claudius Drusus, the driveling imbecile successor to Caligula. But Laughton developed some odd quirks during the early stages of filming. "I had great difficulty managing Laughton," said Sternberg afterwards. "So did Korda; and when Merle Oberon sustained a bad concussion in an automobile accident, which meant so much delay that all our preparations and contracts were invalidated, it was decided to halt the film. It might have been my most successful work. There was no other reason." A comment echoed by Lotte Eisner who, referring to the two reels of *I, Claudius* now reposing in the vaults of the National Film Archives in

London, said it might indeed have become Sternberg's greatest film. Korda, himself, said of this preliminary footage that it was as beautiful as anything he had ever seen on the screen. (It should be noted here that all the stories about Sternberg being a "difficult" and "arrogant" director, like most such stories, were untrue. After the debacle of I, Claudius, Korda wrote Sternberg: "If it is any consolation to you to know, you have left behind you the most loyal and devoted production unit that I have known in connection with any director working for our company [London Films] and should you ever be persuaded to come back and try your hand with us again I know very well that everybody here will be heart and soul with you.")

That same year, Aeneas Mackenzie, writing in Life and Letters Today (London, 1936), in an article titled, "The Leonardo of the Lenses," said, "[His shots], each of which is developed internally . . . detonate into shock, surprise, or startling beauty. And it is by means of this Ford-like internal combustion that a Von Sternberg film progresses in audience interest: before the effect of one emotional percussion has subsided, the next is under way. Consequently, the story does not move his pictures; it is his pictures which move the story."

Recently the British Broadcasting Corporation put together a most unusual film, The Epic That Never Was, a 75-minute documentary on Sternberg's unfinished "cinéma maudit" detailing the contretemps in filming I, Claudius. Filmed in 35mm but primarily for television showing, it is made up in part of interviews with Sternberg, Robert Graves, the costume designer, Merle Oberon, Emlyn Williams (who played Caligula), and Flora Robson (who played the empress-dowager mother of Claudius). Each gives his version of why the film was never completed. The remaining part consists of rushes, as they came from Périnal's camera, of the principal footage shot. It is to be hoped that this film will be made available to television stations and ciné-clubs universally so that audiences may get at least some idea of what this extraordinary project was like.

What was it like?

In some respects it was like the best work of the director, with its ravishing lighting, its silken chiaroscuro, the incandescent softness of the photography in general, especially in the close-ups of faces; also excellence in the acting, especially of Laughton, magnificent as the pitiful Claudius in a long and moving tirade he delivers in the Roman senate defending his right of ascension to the throne. But Emlyn Williams, too, the incarnation of evil as Caligula (there is a single close-up of him worth a hundred lines of the most telling description by the most vivid writer), and the enchanting Merle Oberon in diaphanous veils and bewitching smile that could unnerve a saint, giving youthful promise of the harlot-Messalina she was to become. In short, the complete control over camerawork and direction that we have always known as the hallmark of the director. These images are signed "Sternberg"—you would recognize them as his work even if you did not know beforehand where they came from.

But hold, there is something else—something we have not seen before in Sternberg's films. Or is it the Roman setting, so unusual for Sternberg, that is responsible for our feeling that we have not seen anything like this before from him? In the Temple of Dionysus under a high, vaulted ceiling, pierced by shafts of light from the mid-day sun bathing the enormous enclave in an effulgent luminosity, move worshippers, slowly move the worshippers, their arms outstretched in prayer (shades of Satie's *Gymnopediés*!). The camera, equidistant from the floor of the temple and the ceiling, takes all of this stupendous shot in on one frame, in a single image—and it is breathtaking, *literally* (not figuratively, this time) breathtaking. Nor is a single dimension enough for the director, it never was enough, there always was an overtone to the physical image, a second dimension, a corollary or additional meaning vibrating after the initial "tone" was struck, like "sympathetic harmonies" in music. What Sternberg himself refers to as "*Nachklange*." In this case, it was the awesome sense of the mysticism of the Roman religion. Sternberg has been called everything but never before a mystic. Mysticism is supposed to be the special province of Dreyer, or perhaps Bresson. In this incredible shot, Sternberg is a mystic.

What do the personages interviewed say? Sternberg says least of all. In a few slowly measured words, speaking like a High Lama (so characteristic of him), he dismisses the project philosophically. For him it seemed to be a subject that could not be discussed because it was never completed. Merle Oberon and Flora Robson are voluble, however, especially

Miss Oberon. "Sternberg was chosen because he was considered to be a woman's director," she says. She has much else to say and even jokes about the automobile accident that brought a final halt to the production. Best of all, this Eurasian beauty looks as beautiful as ever, and that's more important than her jocular remarks about "what happened." Flora Robson is still haunted by Sternberg's appearance on the set. "He was the only director I ever saw who really looked like a director," she says. "He would come on the set in riding boots and turban, or even in a silk dressing gown. He was always a little frightening...." She speaks about the miracle of makeup performed on her, transforming her then youthfulness into doddering old age; about the weight of the costumes she had to wear.... At one point Emlyn Williams is cut in right after Sternberg has commented wryly that the automobile accident of Merle Oberon "truncated my film." Says Williams, "Truncated his film? It almost truncated poor Merle!" Referring to Sternberg's difficulties with Laughton, Williams facetiously hazards the guess that the film's producer, Alexander Korda, was himself the chauffeur of the car in which Miss Oberon had the accident, "purposely engineered, probably, to bring an end to the hopeless impasse." The costume designer remarks that he was asked to costume not just six vestal virgins (the number prescribed by Roman ritual as priestesses of the goddess Vesta to tend the sacred fire in her temple), but many times that number because it looked more impressive. Also, that they were to be robed in transparent white tulle revealing their nudity underneath. "Since they were sworn to chastity, it is unlikely," said the costumer, "that they would have been so accoutered. It was all very impressive," he admits (and we see the scene on the screen), "but it had nothing to do with the Roman religion." Robert Graves, author of the book adapted for the film, mutters genially, but has nothing actually to contribute to this "symposium." Only Laughton might have explained, in the face of the reticence of Sternberg to speak, and, alas, this explanation Providence did not vouchsafe us.

The English actor Dirk Bogarde acts as "master of ceremonies" of the BBC film and attempts to fill in the gaps with rumors and hearsay and what sketchy facts have survived the years. So, in the final analysis, only the fragments of the film itself remain, *multum in parvo*, to bear witness to a "beautiful impossibility" that could not for some strange reason be realized, by its very nature, and to remind us in Bacon's words that "there is no excellent beauty that has not some strangeness in the proportion."

While in England, Sternberg planned two other projects, *The Forty Days of Musa Dagh* by Franz Werfel (documenting the grisly Turkish-Armenian aftermath of the First World War) and Zola's *Germinal* (which Pudovkin also once wanted to make). But a recurrence of his illness forced him to abandon both projects and he returned to California.

In January, 1938 he was honored by the Austrian government for furthering Austrian culture and offered the post of director of fine arts in the Austrian ministry, a post he politely declined when it became evident that Hitler was about to annex that country.

In October of that year, MGM offered him a one-picture contract to direct Hedy Lamarr in her second American film, her first, *Algiers*, the remake of *Pepe le Moko*, having been such a success. Although his previous experience with MGM twelve years earlier had been disastrous, he accepted. What was more natural than to think he might do for Hedy Lamarr, certainly the most beautiful screen personality since Dietrich, what he had done for Dietrich? The story, *New York Cinderella*, was by Charles MacArthur and the co-stars were Spencer Tracy and Walter Pidgeon. Harold Rosson was the cameraman. After eight days of shooting, Sternberg and MGM called it quits, again over the issue of the director's freedom, and Frank Borzage was called in to replace him. Borzage's version displeased MGM so much that it was scrapped and entirely reshot by a third director, William S. Van Dyke. Under the title of *I Take This Woman* it was released and went immediately into oblivion. In truth, MGM was a jinx company for Sternberg. He fulfilled his contract for them with another project of their own, *Sergeant Madden*, a tentative return to the *roman policier* type of film with which he had so distinguished himself at Paramount a decade earlier. But his heart wasn't in it—and that always shows.

For two years he was inactive. Then in 1941 the producer Arnold Pressburger decided to revive the idea of filming a sensational play that had resisted all attempts to tame it for the screen—John Colton's *The Shanghai Gesture*, whose setting was a swank Chinese brothel. A violent attack on moral hypocrisy (like Maugham's "Sadie Thompson," which Colton had dramatized as *Rain*), it was an incisive dissection of that tribute (in the irony of La Rochefoucauld) which vice pays to virtue. Sternberg made an adaptation that was both faithful in spirit to the original and could still placate the moral guardians of the American screen.

Sternberg was back in his *milieu* again, with a sympathetic producer, his former directorial freedom, and absolute authority over every department, including the casting. When he offered to send Albert Basserman the script (Sternberg wanted him to play the Police Commissioner), the great German actor replied that he was honored to play in a Sternberg film and it would not be necessary for him to see the script first. For the role of "Mother" Gin Sling (changed from Mother Goddam), Sternberg transformed Ona Munson into a "Chinese Dietrich." The setting, too, was changed, from a brothel, which was then tabu on the sancrosanct American screen, to a high-class gambling house, and several characters were added, including that of Dr. Omar (played by Victor Mature), the Levantine sensualist of shady origins and occupations. Sternberg was fascinated by the many facets of evil displayed by the characters in the Colton melodrama in which the sinners pay their debts, as is the ancient Chinese custom, on the eve of the New Year. The constant return to the huge roulette table in the center of the circular casino, giving the effect of a descent into a maelstrom of iniquity, served as a suggestive pictorial leitmotif throughout the film. And Gene Tierney never looked more beautiful. Originally the film opened with a bearded Sikh policeman directing traffic on a busy intersection of the Shanghai bund, like the conductor of an orchestra. It was, inexplicably, later cut from the film. In any case, the master of *chinoiserie* had done it again. "His strangest and most fascinating work," said *Cahiers du Cinéma*. "I speak in behalf of a whole group of young admirers of your work in Paris," wrote Ado Kyrou to Sternberg, "who consider you as one of the greatest directors that ever lived. We have a huge admiration for your work from *The Salvation Hunters* to the admirable *Shanghai Gesture*. This latest masterpiece of yours is now regularly programmed at the best Parisian ciné-clubs and is passionately discussed at each showing. . . . These audiences are not only sensitive to the magic and metaphysics of the moods so characteristically Sternbergian, but eagerly willing to know analytically of your projects, your plans, and your views about the present cinema."

Whatever the art of the cinema was, it wasn't the "international language of goodwill," nor the ambassador of goodwill," nor the force by which "barriers to mutual understanding" would be overcome, and all the other high-sounding things claimed for it as the cementer of peace between nations. For all the smiles and hand-shaking and bowing at international film festivals, the brotherhood of the cinema was impotent to delay the start of World War II by one second. Refugees began to flee in the wake of the holocaust that was soon to engulf Europe. Among them was the painter, Oskar Kokoschka, whom Sternberg provided with the necessary affidavit to be admitted to the United States with his wife. A touching letter of gratitude from Kokoschka to Sternberg attests to how precious such a document was to the hunted when often it meant the difference between life and death.

When Pearl Harbor was attacked, Sternberg offered his services to the government; later he joined the newly formed OWI (Office of War Information), for which he made a short documentary, *The Town*, on the people in a small Middlewestern community—Madison, Wisconsin. The film was part of a series, "The American Scene." Unlike anything he had ever done before, it showed a great warmth and love for the United States, a film that, during the hysteria of war, eschewed flag-waving patriotism for the positive values of the melting-pot that was the United States. Focusing his camera like a microscope on a tiny segment of this country, he revealed the various foreign elements that went into making the "American way of life." The film (ten minutes long) ended with columns of young soldiers marching out to fight for the security of such an average town and the serenity of its life.

In 1945, Sternberg joined the newly formed Vanguard Films and became consultant to the company's head, David O. Selznick. A year later, while he was serving in an advisory capacity on Selznick's *Duel in the Sun*, he replaced King Vidor briefly, during the latter's illness, as director of the film. (It is an interesting "game" to pick out the scenes that are "*echt*-Sternberg" in this film.)

In 1947, he accepted an appointment at the University of Southern California to teach a class in film direction. The following year he moved to New York.

In 1950 a book appeared in Switzerland, *L'Histoire Universelle*, by Jean Apothéloz, detailing the principal historic events from prehistoric times to that year. Among the historic contributions to the arts was included that of Sternberg.

The year before, Sternberg's former scenarist, Jules Furthman, suggested him for the directorial assignment on Howard Hughes's contemplated aviation epic, *Jet Pilot*. The producer of such box-office successes as *Hell's Angels*, *Two Arabian Knights*, and *The Outlaw* had dabbled in the movies as a rich man's plaything. But his chief business interests involved the manufacture of machine-tools and airplanes. He was himself a considerable flier. Now, for his aviation film, he would consider Sternberg, if the latter shot some "test footage" for him, as if Hughes was interviewing a novice. As if again to disprove the stories of his "arrogance," Sternberg agreed to make a test; which agreement so pleased Hughes that Sternberg was given the assignment. It was to be his first color film. Shooting started in 1950. On its completion, Mr. Hughes decided to cut the film himself. Then he added more flying scenes and recut it. Then still more flying scenes (since flying was *his* obsession, not films), which necessitated still more cutting and rearranging of scenes. Being not only rich but very rich, Mr. Hughes could afford to indulge himself and, because he was young, time didn't matter either. (*Jet Pilot* was not released till 1957.)

While waiting for Hughes to make up his mind about the form in which he would release *Jet Pilot*, Sternberg embarked on the second film of his two-picture contract with Hughes, *Macao*. Despite considerable studio interference, *Macao* was completed by Sternberg in a form that satisfied him. But his satisfaction was to be short-lived. Nicholas Ray was called in to re-shoot the film. The resulting abortion pleased no one, least of all the critics. The film was a critical and box-office fiasco.

"*De l'audace! toujours de l'audace!*" cried Danton. An apt Sternbergian maxim.

No work or project of Sternberg's was ever more audacious

than the book on which he took an option to film next—
Shelby Foote's *Follow Me Down,* a violent tale of a sexual
crime (set in the deep American South) as it is reconstructed
in the bewilderingly conflicting testimony of the witnesses
called on to testify in court . . . a sort of American *Rashomon.*
How Sternberg would have overcome the explicitness of the
sexual details of this cauterizing story will, *hélas,* never be
known. Failing to interest financial backers for the project,
he abandoned it. End of the third phase . . .

We are now in 1952. Sternberg receives an offer to make
a film in Japan, with the guarantee of complete freedom
to make whatever he wishes. (He has always been very popular there. An entire issue of the Japanese magazine *The
Film Critic* [108 pp.] was once devoted to him.) He chooses
a factual incident of the war in the South Pacific concerning a group of Japanese sailors shipwrecked in June 1944 on
the island of Anatahan near Saipan in the Mariana archipelago, who held out there for seven years, refusing to believe
that the war was long since ended and that Japan had been
defeated. Eventually they are convinced, and the survivors
of their intramural fighting over the lone young woman they
found there are returned to the mother country: finally, the
war is over for them. This bizarre incident was turned into
The Saga of Anatahan, for which the director both wrote and
spoke a narration in English over the Japanese dialogue—a
narration that is one of the most searching probes into human
behavior and the mysteries of the human heart that exists
in our time.

The Parisian press was ecstatic. "He has summed up the
vision of the world and the philosophy of existence in it. . . .
From the first image we are again plunged into that famous
enchanted world of Sternberg. It is not only his crowning
achievement but at the same time the best Japanese film,"
wrote *Arts-Spectacles.*

"We are happy to find in this work a Sternberg true to
himself, true to his vision of the world, and true to his old
sorcery," wrote *Le Monde.* "He is behind every image, every
word. A signed film is rare—a film marked by the indelible
print of its author."

"The screen is fairly torn apart and ignited by the fulminations flung upon it, which Von Sternberg, we are sure, drew

from the very depths of his heart. He has won for himself the greatest possible freedom to express a poetic truth and this heightened plane of presentation enhances the radiance of the matter treated. . . . In sum, it is a realization of that kind of work of art considered impossible to accomplish." (*Cahiers du Cinéma*)

In London, Berlin, Switzerland, Australia, and New York the reviews were equally rapturous. And the American Ambassador to Japan, Robert Murphy, congratulated Sternberg on the film.

With *The Saga of Anatahan*, Sternberg had now entered the fourth and final phase of his career—a return to the young artist who had made *The Salvation Hunters*; that is to say, he had regained the complete freedom of expression of his first film, a work of evangelism, a purity of statement without guile, an enunciation of eternal verities. . . . *The Saga of Anatahan*, for all its violence, ends quietly on a brooding note, with just a momentary "flashback" on the sound track of a wisp of remembered passions before the final renunciation of passion is uttered, lowly and wistful, before the Kabuki woodblocks herald the end of the drama . . . "And if I know anything at all about Keiko," concludes the narrator, "she, too, must have been there."

. . .

In 1957 Sternberg is awarded the George Eastman House medal of honor for distinguished contribution to the art of the motion pictures.

In 1960 he is given an "homage" and retrospective showing of his principal films by the Cinémathèque Française.

. . . He is elected an honorary member of the Akademic der Kunst in Berlin, the German counterpart of the Académie Française.

In 1961 he begins a round of the international film festivals, heading the juries at San Francisco, Acapulco, Mar del Plata, Cartagena, Locarno, Cannes, Venice, Vienna, and Berlin. He lectures at universities in Colombia and Argentina.

1962 . . . He is cited by the Museum of Performing Arts of San Francisco for his "consistently significant and artistic contributions rendered to the world of the performing arts and for enriching the culture of our time."

. . . *Show* magazine in New York runs a symposium of

distinguished foreigners who have contributed to American culture: "To make progress," said the introduction, "every culture must periodically recapture the exhilaration of danger, what Kierkegaard called 'the passionate expectancy' of the committed man." The list included Dali, Adler, Gropius, Breuer, Mann, Teller, Fermi, Einstein, Ernst, Neutra, Nabokov, Mies van der Rohe, and two film names—Stroheim and Sternberg.

1963 . . . Jorge Luis Borges, the greatest living Spanish writer, mentions the influence of Sternberg's films on his work in the foreword to his novel *La Muerta y la Brujula*.

. . . He is honored by the West German government for "his services to the German film industry" (for *The Blue Angel*, made 34 years before).

. . . He is honored by the Mexican government for his artistic and humanist contributions to the cinema.

1964 . . . Retrospective showings of his films and tributes are given him by the University of California and Dartmouth College.

. . . He lectures at universities in Minnesota, California, Illinois, Iowa, and at Notre Dame College.

. . . Walter Starkie, professor of Spanish, Irish, and Italian literature and former director of the Abbey Theatre in Dublin, testifies in a tribute given Sternberg at the University of California in Los Angeles that Shaw, Pirandello, Joyce, and Lorca admired and often discussed his films.

1965 . . . He teaches a film directing course at U.C.L.A. in California.

. . . He begins the revision of an autobiography on which he has been working for several years. Originally called *Guide to a Labyrinth*, it appears in 1965 as *Fun in a Chinese Laundry*.

Just as in the first part of *Faust*, the protagonist has not yet found, in the world of desire and passion, that wonderful moment of existence to which he could really wish to cling, but finds it in the second part when, after tasting every form of intellectual and worldly power, he turns to good works, taking an interest in a project to reclaim land from the sea, a project which will mean little to him, personally, but which will bring untold good to countless others, so did Sternberg turn from the clamorous world of Hollywood and its glitter to a threnody that is at the same time an affirmation of life,

The Saga of Anatahan, for which his only reward has been the elation it has given others *sans* any material reward to himself.

1966 . . . Retrospective showing of his films at Mannheim, Germany, at which is issued a 200-page "documentation" of his complete work.

1967 . . . Retrospective showing of his films in Stockholm and Sydney.

.   .   .

In a *milieu* with its easy contempt for aesthetic values, the hieratic disdain of his style—which ranks with the most patrician filmmaking in the world—is a thrilling thing to see, as it always is wherever work is touched, "beyond the call of duty," with the vital grace of art.

II

"To know what to reveal and what to conceal is the secret of art."

"Everything I have to say about Miss Dietrich I have said with the camera."

—Josef von Sternberg

A discussion of "Sternberg and Marlene" has its origins in the mists of antiquity, its roots in Hellenic culture, "the Greek miracle," before Pan disappeared into the forests, never to be seen again. The great poets that followed Homer invented a mythology based on the ancient Greek religion that illumined what the early Greeks were like, a matter of importance to us, who are their descendants intellectually and artistically. Nothing we learn about them is alien to ourselves. The whole of Western civilization owes its genesis to the ancient Greeks, and Herodotus limns them succinctly when he says, "Of old the Hellenic race was marked off from the barbarian as more keen-witted and more free from nonsense." Whereas the Egyptians represented their goddesses in unhuman form, a woman with a cat's head or a monstrous, mysterious sphinx, Greek mythology humanized the world, freeing men from the paralyzing fear of an omnipotent Unknown. The men who made the myths disliked the irrational and had a love for facts, no matter how wildly fantastic some of the stories are. They occur in a world that is essentially rational and matter-of-fact. Although the ethical background of these tales is religious, many are nonreligious and have to do with explaining natural phenomena, thus becoming a kind of early science. Better than that, they were highly poetic. Some explained nothing at all, being tales of pure entertainment, springing solely from the human heart and its limit-less fantasies, such as the tale Ovid tells of Pygmalion and Galatea. Like the legend of Orpheus and Eurydice, it has no conceivable connection with nature or religion. Such tales were written as pure entertainment, becoming at the same time the first literature.

Pygmalion and Galatea.* . . . Perhaps in no artist–creation relationship of the twentieth century is the spirit of this im-mortal tale more vividly exemplified than in the Sternberg–Marlene relationship in the seven (ah, seven, that old mystical number!) films he made of her. I purposely do not say "with her"—but "of her"—because seven times he, too, "sculpted" her—as did Pygmalion sculpt Galatea, making seven versions of an ideal, each time refining the vision he had of her, adding a detail here, subtracting one there, revealing a facet of her "eternal mystery" here, concealing one there, until the sum total, which is to say, the final creation, was ex-quisite. Both Pygmalion and Sternberg labored long and devotedly on their creation but did not rest content. Under their skilled fingers it grew more and more beautiful. No woman ever born, no representation of a woman ever made, could approach it. Ovid does not tell us how long Pygmalion worked on his Galatea. Sternberg worked five years on his. Only in one way did they differ: The well-spring of Pyg-malion's art was his hatred of women: "Detesting the faults beyond measure which nature has given to women," in the words of Ovid. Thus, resolving never to marry, Pygmalion embarked on the sculpture of a woman, the perfect woman, to show men the deficiencies of the kind they had to put up with. With Sternberg it was different. He may not have

* Sternberg's first Galatea was a wax mannikin in a short story published by him in 1924, *The Waxen Galatea*, that was to presage things to come. A shy man falls desperately in love with a mannikin in the window of a women's fashion shop. Day after day he gazes with adoration on this inert figure of wax, wrapt in silent rapture at her indefatigable grace of gesture, marveling at the gown which draped her nudity. One day the unhappy man sees passing in the street the living image of his goddess. He follows her but she has a rendezvous with another man who, at the woman's request, humili-ates her adorer who has become an irksome intruder on her rendez-vous. Dismayed, he removes himself, deciding never again to take the risk, in the future, of loving anyone more than the mannikin.

thought much of them as actresses (nor of men as actors) without a sensitive director's guiding hand, but for women as women he had the highest respect. This is borne out by the films of his pre-Dietrich period, long before he met her, in his treatment of Georgia Hale, Edna Purviance, Evelyn Brent, Betty Compson, and Esther Ralston—every one of them portrayed sympathetically, as loyal companions of their men. Even in his own A.D. period, "After Dietrich," his attitude remained constant in his equally sympathetic handling of Marian Marsh, Ona Munson, Gene Tierney, Janet Leigh, Jane Russell, and Akemi Negishi. There are no villainesses in the films of Von Sternberg, not even Lola-Lola of *The Blue Angel*, who describes her problem in the song she sings the night the Professor visits her cabaret:

"Men flutter round me like moths around a flame,
And if they get burned then, well, I am not to blame."

But the Professor does not heed the warning. His head is turned by the odor of musk and civet she exudes for him. He is consumed in the flame, being unable to cope with this reality, victim of a sexual drive he never faced before, and run over by it.

And, as Edith Hamilton, that great Greek scholar, goes on to say, in retelling the story of Pygmalion, "When nothing could be added to the statue's perfection, a strange fate befell its creator: he had fallen in love, deeply, passionately in love, with the thing he had made. It must be said in explanation that the statue did not look like a statue; no one would have thought it was ivory or stone, but warm human flesh, motionless for a moment only. Such was the wondrous power of this disdainful young man. *The supreme achievement of art was his, the art of concealing art."* (Italics mine.) Does Sternberg depart again from Pygmalion in this respect? We are free to believe it or not. The truth is beside the point; such is the nature of art that it transcends homely truths. The things great or beautiful done by men are greater or more beautiful than they are. They would not be *great* artists or scientists or whatever if their work did not transcend themselves. That goes for Nietzsche, himself, who said just the opposite, that nothing in itself is beautiful: man, alone, is beautiful. It is beautiful only because *he* is there to admire it. Which only goes to show that opposites can be one, for this statement is not so opposite after all.

The Blue Angel posed its own problems for Sternberg, a whoop-dee-do which had to be set within the limitations of the characters of the impudent Lola-Lola and the fool Professor. Sternberg etches his *dramatis personae* swiftly, like a newspaper or magazine caricaturist doing his regular stint for, let us say, *Simplicissimus*, the acidly brilliant satirical weekly that flourished in Germany up to the advent of Hitler. He is *engagé* by the erotic appeal of the plump, pretty dumpling he finds in Dietrich, as perfectly suited in his mind for the cantharidic lubricity of this brazen Berlin tart, baiting the customers of a third-rate dive—we can almost smell the stale beer, tobacco smoke, and sweat of this sleazy cabaret. *The Blue Angel* was the most realistic German film since *Variety* with hymeneal hymns to priapic exploits (as in the coarse ditty, "Tonight, Fellows, I'm Looking for a Real Man"). He senses the animal breath of her sensual person but no one but he does. Until then she was a minor actress in some minor films and stage revues. And even after he introduces her to Pommer and Jannings at Ufa as a *fait accompli*, the Lola-Lola to-be of *The Blue Angel*, no one but he can smell this animal breath. Of course, by the time he finished the picture, and it knocked a gala opening night audience into stupefaction, they smelled it too. But Sternberg didn't wait to see the effect of the film on audiences; he returned to Hollywood, knowing full well the havoc he had done, and determined to consolidate this accomplishment with Dietrich's first American film. It was she who gave him the romantic novel to read on the boat returning to New York, *Amy Jolly*, by an obscure writer, Benno Vigny. It was this that Sternberg decided had the germ of an idea for her American debut, which he would call *Morocco*.

The sleek and mysterious Amy Jolly of *Morocco* was a far cry from the buxom trollop of *The Blue Angel*, as different as the two stories themselves were. For *Morocco*, Sternberg abandoned the realistic style of *The Blue Angel* for the "glamorous style" of Hollywood. Marlene had been signed by Paramount to a long-term contract, she had to be groomed to the American taste and the American taste called for glamour—not realism. (For a realistic picture of the

Foreign Legion, see Feyder's *Le Grande Jeu* or Duvivier's *La Bandera*.) Sternberg saw to this. Master of many styles, he set a tone for Marlene's American debut that suited her so well that he was unable to free himself from involvement in it. "After my second picture with Marlene," he said, "I did not want to make any more films with her. But Miss Dietrich said to me, 'You want to show the world you're a great director and that I am a bad actress. Isn't that what you want to do? You want me to go to another director.' Being a gentleman, I continued."

It is very disconcerting to interview Sternberg. He pretends you know the right questions to ask, the pertinent ones, and it's almost impossible to think of a right question when you consider the answers you get to those you do ask. When Stephen Watts in London in the late Thirties interviewed him in an article captioned: "The Truth About Dietrich and von Sternberg," the director was quoted: "If I had not brought out Miss Dietrich's qualities [he always refers to her, with the barest exceptions, as "Miss Dietrich"], somebody else would have done so six months later. I played the part of an abstract destiny, rather than a discoverer. She was grateful—not sentimentally, but with an intellectual gratitude. . . ."

Then: "We went on making films together because we were forced to. I did it reluctantly. From my own point of view as a director, I was through with Miss Dietrich after *Morocco*. I had made *The Blue Angel* in Germany showing her in one mood, and in Hollywood I tried the experiment of showing her in a lazier, more exotic style. I had no more experiments in mind and she had no need of me. . . ."

Finally: "But we were made to go on, protesting, until at last I refused to plagiarize myself anymore."

Selah! These are the facts and facts are stubborn things, you cannot argue with them. But what do they tell us of the "mysterious" *rapport* in this unique example of director and star, absolutely unique in the annals of the screen? Of the influence they had on each other? There are aesthetic truths that are truer than facts. "Art is a lie," said Picasso, "that helps us see the truth." Then we must go back to the films, themselves, for the answer. Or, before doing so, we can recall some of Dietrich's own statements on the subject of her mentor: After completing their last film together, *The Devil Is a Woman*, she was quoted by a London interviewer

(Charles Graves, in *The Daily Sketch*) as saying: "He is by far the greatest director in the world. I would love to be in one of his pictures again—even in a small part." On another occasion: "If anyone says anything against him, I have nothing to say to such a person, I don't even see this person, I look right through him."

Let's try going back to the films for a clue . . .

The Czech novelist, Max Brod, in *Die Frau nach der man sich sehnt* (*The Woman You Are Yearning For*)—in which Dietrich co-starred with Fritz Kortner and Uno Henning in Germany a year before *The Blue Angel* (a 1929 silent film directed by Kurt Bernhardt)—has for its theme the "ideal" woman of a man's dreams. Dietrich prophetically played this role, for she was to become the consummation of a dream long held some 6000 miles from Berlin by a young director in Hollywood in whom, in the women he chose for his films, there seemed to be a groping for some quality he wanted but only fitfully obtained and that never fully. Study the sullen face of Georgia Hale in *The Salvation Hunters*, with its weary glances, and see how it is repeated in the faces of Evelyn Brent in *Underworld*, *The Dragnet*, and *The Last Command*, and again by Betty Compson in *Docks of New York*. These are all world-weary women, searching, themselves, for something they want. Never once does a nimbus shine from them, never once do they light up the screen with a radiance —why? Because the director has not yet been inspired by them. They are all very attractive and play their parts well, but you feel that the director is not inspired by them. They don't catch fire because the director hasn't caught fire. He is doing magnificent jobs on the pictures, but his women stars don't "send" him, as the saying goes. But you sense that he is feeling his way and you hope with him that some day he will find her. He seemingly abandons the search in his choice of the very sympathetic Esther Ralston for *The Case of Lena Smith* . . . and a thoroughly colorless Fay Wray in *Thunderbolt*, both in 1929, bridging the transition from the silent film to sound with the latter . . .

And then came the invitation from Erich Pommer, of Ufa, via Emil Jannings's recommendation, to come to Berlin.

Sternberg has said that the image he had in mind for Lola-Lola had already been drawn by the acidulous French artist, Félicien Rops. When he found her that night at a performance of Georg Kaiser's play, *Zwei Krawatten* (*Two Neck-ties*), she "was not only a model who had been designed by Rops, but Toulouse-Lautrec would have turned a couple of handsprings had he laid eyes on her." Obviously, with two such mordant artist-*flâneurs* as her spiritual "godfathers" in the mind of the director, two such acrid observer-denizens of the *demi-monde*, she would be ideal as the tawdry saloon singer of Heinrich Mann's story, capable of leading that "pillar of respectability," Professor Immanuel Rat, by the nose. But what initially attracted the director to her was the "cold disdain" that emanated from her presence on the stage that night, her "impressive poise." He had not only found his Lola-Lola, he had found something more, much more, as it turned out to be. Was he aware of that at the time? Again, we can believe it or not. Sternberg had already changed the name of the heroine, if that's the word for her, from the novel's Rosa Froehlich to Lola-Lola, inspired by Wedekind's Lulu in *Pandora's Box*. If it was just a ques-tion of settling for the right Lola-Lola, well, that wouldn't necessarily have taken too long—Berlin had many attractive young actresses who could have been manipulated by a clever director every-which-way. Hadn't Pabst imported Louise Brooks from Hollywood for his film of *Pandora's Box*. And, after an immediate follow-up second picture with her, hadn't he sent her back to Hollywood? He saw only Lulu in her, no-thing else. (Even in *Diary of a Lost One* she still was Lulu.) But Sternberg did see something else in Dietrich, something that was to change both their lives and careers for the next five years. *Morocco*, the second film he made with her, was utterly different from *The Blue Angel*, as was Amy Jolly from Lola-Lola. Now he refined her screen image and now a nimbus radiated from her and she shined on the screen with a radiant light. The old sullenness was back, the weary glance, the world-weariness of his first screen women—only now he *was* inspired, now he painted her with soft lights and shadows, now he had a star on whose face he could lavish his treasure, the limitless knowledge he had of light-ing and photography. If ever the camera caressed the face of a star, it did so in the films they made together. Erwin, the hero of Brod's novel, had found his Stasha, the woman he was yearning for, Pygmalion had found his Galatea. Of course, he wanted to leave her after *Morocco*; of course, she refused. The gods who attend these things smile at human bickerings and give them just enough leeway to let them think they are creatures of free will. Paramount was appointed by them the *deus ex machina* of this *comédie humaine*. A poet a thousand years ago wrote, "On the first day of creation was set down what the last day of reckoning will read." There is no such thing as chance, then; it is fate, misnamed . . . so they say.

Now this is all terribly romantic, I know, but how else do you write on the subject of "Sternberg and Marlene"? Good films, like all other good art, are not made in a vacuum. They spring from real thoughts, real feelings. You can be as objective as you like, but you cannot hide it, though you may disguise it. At the risk of compounding one error into two, I repeat: "There are aesthetic truths that are truer than the facts."

We have remarked on the uniqueness of this director–star relationship. It was in truth unique. You cannot compare the Czinner–Bergner director–star relationship with it for, though for a long while Paul Czinner directed only Elisabeth Bergner, there were two differences: (a) she was his wife; (b) she always played the same part, at least for a long time she did; the child–woman. The same goes for Godard and Anna Karina. Stiller–Garbo? One picture together, though it meant something more to him than that. Who else? Antonioni–Vitti? Romantic only to themselves. . . .

Another point. In connection with my earlier musings on the women in Sternberg's first films, it is interesting to note that, when being interviewed by him for *The Blue Angel*, Dietrich informed the director that she had seen some of his previous work, and, though she reluctantly conceded that he knew how to handle men, she doubted that he could do as well with women. When Merle Oberon was interviewed by the BBC in London for *The Epic That Never Was*, you will recall that Miss Oberon volunteered the information that Sternberg was chosen by Alexander Korda to direct *I, Claudius* because he had become famous as a "woman's director." (Miss Oberon was married to Mr. Korda at the time.) This was, of course, *after* the Dietrich films. Richard Griffith, former curator of the Museum of Modern Art Film Library, quotes "a not entirely bemused observer," C. H. Rand: "I know well enough, of course, that the enchantment is not Marlene alone. I see her through the eyes of Josef von Sternberg, Like all the great screen characters, Marlene is a myth, a symbol, an idea. And it is because she is the perfect embodiment of that idea that she has this fascination for me. As with all men, a fair part of my subconscious life spends itself in a dream of a perfect vamp. I want a woman whose passion is not a blind rage of the body or the soul, but a recognition of mutual attraction in which reason or humor will play their part, as far as love permits. But vamps with brains are far to seek. And vamps with humor even further. I find all my requisites in the screen character of Marlene Dietrich. She has beauty in abundance. She has a rich, sensuous allure. And you have only to look at her eyes to see that she has brains, and at her mouth to see that she has humor."

Bien sur, it is exactly these qualities which she has in her Sternberg films, and in no other, in absolutely no other. Most of the characters in the films of Von Sternberg are mouthpieces for the director—they say what he would say in their places, male or female, it makes no difference. He wrote all their dialogue, anyway. Often, they speak like he does, in slow, measured cadences, or with dry, deadpan wit. Sometimes they even look like him, as Lionel Atwill did as Don Pasquale in *The Devil Is a Woman*.

"Out of this matrix of legend," continues Richard Griffith, "sprang two mutually contradictory ones, each in its own way, like Freudian dreamwork, trying to account for the prominence of the screen Marlene. Believing she would work with no other director, it was for a long time almost universally believed that Marlene Dietrich and Josef von Sternberg constituted a Trilby and Svengali of the studios, with the star under the hypnotic domination of the director, much to her own detriment: this legend held that Von Sternberg was merely using Dietrich and her great popularity as a prop to enable him to indulge his taste for pictorial extravagance, Dietrich being to him no more than a red thread in the elaborate visual pattern of his films. The opposing legend, subscribed to by the much smaller number of the director's admirers, was that his obsession with Marlene was destroying him as an artist. How else to account for his exclusive concentration on her, at the expense of the narrative and dramatic aspects of their films? Here was a superb director, potentially second to none, enslaved to an image! To no one—including this writer—does it seem to have occurred at the time that it is not only the business but the golden privilege of a film director to create great images, and that in Marlene Dietrich Von Sternberg knew that he had made the discovery of a lifetime."

Have we said that Dietrich took a real interest in the techniques of filmmaking, of the lighting and photography in particular? Being intelligent and having, herself, artistic sensibility, she was frequently helpful. "She was a good assistant," said Sternberg. They worked, as the saying goes, "hand in glove." There was never a better fit,

Between *The Blonde Venus* and *The Scarlet Empress*, which is to say, after five pictures in a row with Sternberg, she made *The Song of Songs* with Rouben Mamoulian at Sternberg's suggestion. "It will do you good to work with another director, for a change," he said. As the heroine of Hermann Sudermann's novel she played an innocent peasant girl who meets a famous sculptor who asks her to model a nude statue of the ideal of feminine loveliness. She does and he falls in love with her. Pygmalion and Galatea again? Let us not make too much of this analogy despite its persistence, though why shouldn't we note here that Sternberg was a sculptor, too, not just metaphorically, but actually? One of his works is a striking nude female torso—with a rosary.

Finally, who had the greater influence on whom? Sternberg would have been Sternberg and everything that that connotes even without Dietrich. He was that long before he met her, and in the fragments of *I, Claudius*, in *The Shanghai Gesture* and *Anatahan*, he was still that even without her. She was nothing before she met him and only occasionally interesting after the two broke up, very occasionally, and even then almost completely without the humor and *panache* with which she played under Sternberg. For instance, her Concha in *The Devil Is a Woman* is played on the highest level of wit, a devastating parody of the whole idea of the *femme fatale*, a type of role she and Sternberg raised to the highest comic (but most telling) degree, the apogee of what Renoir strove for in Catherine Hessling's stylized playing of the title role in his *Nana*. (As a contrast of how you do this when you're in dead earnest, one could cite the way the vamp is portrayed in Renoir's *La Chienne*.)

And apropos *The Devil Is a Woman*, this sado-masochistic story, played in that vein to the nth power, do we not find in this extraordinary swan-song of its director–star collaboration a clue to the fire that activated their seven films together? It is their favorite film. It is a summing up of everything they went through together, in and out of the studio. Both knew it was to be their last together and they made their ultimate statements on this relationship in it. This was more than a Svengali–Trilby affair, if it ever was that, for it was bruited that this Trilby also had a hypnotic effect on her Svengali. If so, this paradox would fit in with the characteristically perverse humor with which the Sternberg–Dietrich films are rife. (Like the lesbian joke in *Morocco*, for instance, or the delicate goddess emerging from the horrendous gorilla costume in *The Blonde Venus*.) A psychoanalyst might flippantly hazard the guess that it was Trilby who hypnotized Svengali, rather than the other way around, though, of course, Svengali never realized that. He could make quite a case for it, *after the fact*, of course, since you can rationalize almost anything, given the smallest "fulcrum and a place to stand" to paraphrase Archimedes.

But enough of this game. Let the marvelous epiphanies these two created together for whatever reason (the elements that go into the making of a work of art must always, in the last analysis, remain a mystery) suffice us.

"Dietrich never influenced me," says Sternberg. "I influenced her. Her stature absorbed what I had to offer. In that respect she was good."

And Pygmalion, in the legend as Ovid tells it, what happened to him? Oh, it all ended banally enough. Venus took pity on his pinings over the statue and brought it to life. With unutterable gratitude and joy he put his arms around his love and saw her smile into his eyes and blush. Venus herself graced their marriage with her presence. They had a son and lived happily ever after, *pardee*!

But that has nothing to do with the cinema.

III

The Salvation Hunters opens with a sea gull perched on a piece of flotsam floating in Los Angeles bay and *Anatahan* ends on a Japanese airfield. Between these two far-flung images is a span of 28 years, during which Sternberg completed 22 films (John Ford made 129), of which 18 are still available for re-viewing and re-evaluation today. *Woman of the Sea* is owned by Chaplin, who has made no copy available to any cinémathèque. *The Dragnet* and *The Case of Lena Smith* are similarly not to be found in any cinémathèque. *Jet Pilot*, even in its mutilated released form, is also unavailable for re-viewing, being owned by the elusive Howard Hughes, who has apparently withdrawn it from circulation. And of these 18, three may be dismissed as having been made under unfelicitous conditions—*Crime and Punishment, The King Steps Out*, and *Sergeant Madden*. Remains 15 . . .

What do these 15 films say to us today that is still cogent? Certainly, the world of 1967 is different from the one a generation ago—1925—that witnessed the birth of Sternberg's art. Seeing them today, in the midst of all the new films, they look so different as to seem to have been made on another planet. (Or maybe it is the new films that look so different that *they* seem to have been made on another planet—anyway, both do not come from the same world.) And not only Sternberg's films but those of all that hallowed company of his colleagues in the cinema pantheon as well. And why is this? Because there has been no transition. Here we have the one serious lack in the cinema as a continuing art that is present in all the other arts, e.g., the continuity of tradition through the flowering of disciples. This is present not only in all other creative arts but in the performing arts as well. Only the cinema has no traditions that are maintained, and its "old masters," the first ones, the

Giottos of the film, have no disciples. Some of them exerted a brief influence, chiefly because those influences were a vogue of the moment, but when that vogue was over these influences disappeared. Most of them had no influence at all. The stronger the individuality of the artist in the cinema, the less influence he usually exerts, because the idea of disciples is not natural to the cinema. On the rare occasions when it happened, it was self-willed and this will had to be imposed on the film industry, for it never meant to be an art but an industry. It became an art despite itself by stubborn self-willed artists who imposed themselves on this industry. This is the only salutary tradition of the cinema— the will of the artist. The "Western" flowered in America because individuality of statement did not matter in this *genre*. Bad "Westerns" were as rare as good "Westerns," the general level of acceptable competence being on such a low plane. The triumph of this *genre* is the triumph of mediocrity—always the safest and surest level on which to work. In the very beginning, Griffith, Mack Sennett, Chaplin, Stroheim, Murnau, and Lubitsch (in his early American films) can be said to have had some disciples for a while during the formative years of the motion pictures. But this did not last or develop except sporadically and with increasingly less frequency. Who were the disciples of the apocalyptic visions of the Lang of the *Nibelungen* and *Metropolis*, the Gance of *J'Accuse* and *Napoleon*, of that most cerebral of film poets, Eisenstein? Who was the disciple of the Dreyer of *La Passion de Jeanne d'Arc*? Of course it was perfectly natural that new talents would develop over the years in a new medium that was "catching on" so popularly. But if we are mindful that the word, disciple, comes from discipline, which is to say, the training that develops self-control, character, orderliness, and efficiency, even those new talents (when they *were* talented) who wanted to go their own way could not bypass the rules of film grammar and syntax with which the film language had been initially formed. And style, too, if it was to be followed, or copied, or to serve as an inspiration, it, too, had its rules of weights and balances, its limits of interplay beyond which the interplay would lose itself in irrelevancies; most of all it had its celebration of indigenously cinematic epiphanies, *vide*, Renoir's *Nana* or Ford's *My Darling Clementine*, to take two disparate examples. Would there have been the Soviet *New Babylon* without this *Nana* to show it the way? Yesterday, Renoir was idolized by the French New Wave but no one is following in his footsteps. There are many roads to Parnassus but you have to at least be *on* the road, if that's where you're headed for. Who makes those roads? Every new creative artist with a vision of his own who does not see his personal vision on the horizon of an already existing path. He uses the same tools to climb that path but he carries his own banner, his style. And he is subject to the laws of artistic gravity and aesthetic equilibrium once he is on that path (e.g., discipline) and must beware the pitfalls of imbalance or he will fall. The eclectics, like Orson Welles, are bound by the same unity and harmony of purpose that binds them all, all those who would reach Parnassus, where Apollo and the Muses dwell. The poets, like Vigo, Clair, and Cocteau, do not even have to climb, they are winged . . . But every true artist is a poet or he would not even be looking toward Parnassus but at the box office.

All of which is by way of introduction to the fact that Sternberg's films, like those of all the "old masters," do not exist in a vacuum, nor are they today like hot-house flowers that must be artificially nurtured to retain their bloom. The bloom will forever be on them. What made them exceptional in their time is what gives them their staying power today, and those qualities are still, and always will be, exceptional. The cogency of those films for us today is in their validity of statement and the technique with which that statement was made, the formal discipline that guided that technique, and its obeisance to the immutable laws of aesthetics, for this is a part of the statement, just like the editing of a film is a part of the direction. In short—the way a story is told is part of that story. You can tell the same story badly or well; you can also tell it well enough or magnificently. It depends on who is telling the story. That is perhaps why form is, in the last analysis, as Freud pointed out, of more decisive importance than content, though under ideal conditions the latter dictates the style of the former. There is always one best way to tell a story and that way has to be found. "The difference between the right word and the almost-right word," said Mark Twain, "is the difference between lightning and a fire-fly."

Let us begin our critical "re-evaluation" of Sternberg today by briefly examining first his influence. *Underworld,* as we have noted, had a decided influence in catapulting a new *genre*—the gangster film—in America. Not only did he introduce a new theme (always a rarity) to the American screen but even something of his laconic style seeped into the plethora of gangster films that followed (*Quick Millions, Scarface, Doorway to Hell, The Public Enemy, Little Caesar*). But having said that, it is difficult to find further influences save in single occasional works here and there. If Mamoulian owed *Love Me Tonight* to Lubitsch, he certainly owed *The Song of Songs* to Sternberg, but only pictorially—the harshness and sardonic edge of Sternberg, which was his strength beyond his exotic pictorialism, was missing. Nicholas Farkas's *La Bataille,* especially in its English version (*Thunder in the East,* with Boyer, Inkijinoff, Merle Oberon, and John Loder) is a "Sternbergian" film, and certainly Ozep's *Der Moerder Karamazov* is almost *echt*-Sternberg throughout—the only film I know from another director that I would not have been surprised to see signed by him. I mean this as a compliment to Ozep. I cannot think of another, offhand, until Welles's *Lady from Shanghai,* especially for its elliptical style, so characteristic of the director of *Underworld* and *Morocco,* and its penchant for *bizarrerie.* Although Sternberg did not attach much importance to the dialogue in his sound films, regarding it chiefly as intonations, as part of the sound, like the individual notes of a music score have importance not singly but only as part of an orchestration, it is interesting to notice that the dialogue in his films, for all that, is invariably highly literate and sophisticated. This quality is to be found also in the Farkas, Ozep, and Welles illustrations above cited. Since then there has been nothing I know of traceable to Sternberg's work, although I have heard that Jacques Demy (in *Lola* and *The Bay of Angels*) is regarded as fitfully reflecting Sternberg's influence, an observation I reject without prejudice to Demy. So much for Sternberg's influence . . .

One of the reasons for the lack of films influenced by his work is their daring, both technical and ideological. He took risks, not out of bravado (the plane of his intelligence was always too high for that) but because his *daemon* impelled him toward it; it was as if it were *inevitable* that he do it. The inexorable logic of *Morocco*, since it is a true love story, is that, if it has to come to that, one risks all for love. And just as Amy Jolly leaves the rich LeBessière to follow her Legionnaire into the desert,* at which bourgeois audiences laugh because they would never do such a foolish thing, least of all for love, Sternberg, too, hazards the same risk his heroine does because he, too, has done it for the same reason. Both have been true to themselves—hence their actions were inevitable. Proust, in his preface to Paul Morand's *Green Shoots*, admires his stylistic brilliance but finds one fault—that Morand's imagery is *not always inevitable*. This is the heart of the matter. One does not cavil with the first rule of human conduct—"Know thyself." And just as most audiences would not have followed Amy Jolly's action, most directors would not be apt to follow Sternberg's. Maybe they knew themselves, also, and their selves were different. But note that the three illustrations cited as possibly being influenced by Sternberg carry the same convictions. In *Thunder in the East*, the Japanese naval commander commits *hara kiri* because he feels he has dishonored himself through his wife, although he dearly loves her. In *Der Moerder Karamazov*, Grushinka willingly follows Dmitri on a prison train to Siberia for ten years because, as she says, "People love in Siberia, too." In *Lady from Shanghai*, the hero allows himself to become involved with a sinister character in a plot that, if successful, might make it possible for him to run off with the young woman he's in love with. He knows he is playing with fire but is willing to risk it. Audiences in their snug seats and directors in their snug berths are disturbed by such seeming self-sacrifices and laugh them off in self-protection. But Sternberg could well say with Gide, "To disturb, that is my role."

Who would dare to follow the director of such paroxysmic explosions of the baroque as *The Scarlet Empress* and *The Devil Is a Woman*? (You can only make such films—and get away with them—once.) Who would become a disciple of a director who follows a film in which the action pivots around a dredge scooping up mud from a river bottom (*The*

---

* Much has been made of the "absurdity" of this scene where Amy Jolly goes into the desert on high heels. Unperceptive critics as well as audiences failed to notice that after a few impulsive steps she kicks her heels off.

Salvation Hunters), and whose characters are the dregs of the earth, with one that was so physically beautiful (*Woman of the Sea*) that its producer was bewildered by it and refused to release it? How do you follow a director who then makes six harsh films in a row, each getting progressively harsher and more bitter, from *Underworld* to *The Blue Angel*, among them the unforgettable *Docks of New York*, which rivals *Woman of the Sea* in beauty of photography and poetry of motion, although half the action takes place either in the stoke-hole of a dirty tramp steamer or a sordid waterfront saloon, and then follows this with a romantic film so unique in its use of sound against image (*Morocco*) as to still be, thirty-seven years later, one of the supreme examples of utilizing the best elements of both the silent and the sound film? Not only would the prospective disciple be bewildered by such versatility but to follow in the footsteps of Sternberg he would have to come up with something original and unprecedented of his own, too, all the while. It is not just a matter of copying Sternberg's glistening photography. The usually perceptive John Grierson made one of the silliest statements in film history when, after praising the photography of *Woman of the Sea*, he concluded wistfully, "When a director dies he becomes a photographer." The very next film Sternberg made was *Underworld*, which catapulted him into overnight fame as a director. The disciple would also have to have such control over every element of his film as has been vouchsafed few directors in what has become increasingly a producer's medium, rather than the director's. Who would dare such a shot as the train getting under way in the beginning of *Shanghai Express*, slowly chugging its way through a narrow Chinese street so crowded with people as to make one wonder if such a thing were possible? Directors more timid and more discreet would not hazard such an "unrealistic" scene—with their usual banal results, *bien entendu*. Sternberg throws discretion to the winds where it serves his artistic purpose. He reserves discretion for where it belongs—in the relations between his characters. How better to get across the idea of a "China teeming with people" than the way he does it? The essence of reality is better than reality, where art is concerned. Both Goethe and Picasso have attested to this as an aesthetic principle. Renoir's Nana was not like Zola's, and neither was like the real Nana, for there was a real Nana. But what does it matter? Only the idea matters and that is the function of art. In the words of Klee, "Art does not reproduce the visible, it *makes* visible." When the chant from the muezzin calls the faithful to prayer in *Morocco*, the Arabs under the *soukh* fall to their knees and bend down, but not all of them (though any other director would have had all of them)—two Arabs walk away from the camera and the shadows of the overhanging trellises that form the *soukh* glide with delicate tracery across their white robes. Sternberg gives us something to enchant the eye while the song of prayer is going on, but even this isn't done gratuitously, for the moment of prayer serves to introduce the leading character, Gary Cooper, as the Legionnaire, who uses the preoccupation of the Arabs to make an assignation in pantomime with a native girl eyeing him from a doorway. And even this isn't all; the handsome Cooper's devastating effect on women is laconically stated a moment before when a young Arab woman from a low rooftop lets down her veil for a second to reveal her prettiness to him. All of this rich detail while the muezzin chant is going on takes less than half a minute of screen time. This is how you direct, this is how you avoid soul-destroying waits between things happening (for screen-time is highly concentrated and fifteen seconds of watching someone read a letter on the screen can make a misanthrope out of an angel), this is how you employ cinematic polyphony, as a composer does in musical composition. The inter-cutting of several images and sounds to orchestrate a scene to its fullest plangency, all contributing to the story, plot-wise or nuance-wise (no nuance is so delicate that it cannot enrich a scene), is one of Sternberg's most characteristic effects (*vide* his *"reaction"* scenes in *Vanity's Price* mentioned earlier). *Morocco*, that endlessly fascinating source of felicitous screen direction, opens polyphonically with two opposing actions—a column of Legionnaires marching from the far distance into a town to the arrogant beat of their drums—and, as they approach nearer and nearer, an Arab in the foreground struggling frantically to get his donkey off the road, cursing the stubborn animal and his forebears. The Arab's exasperated fulminations are like a farrago of crazy arpeggios over the inexorably approaching drum beats, getting louder and louder. Humor and suspense from the first frame. Just in time, the Arab manages

The die is cast. Dietrich prepares to go on for her American début in the memorable café scene of *Morocco*. Paul Porcasi as the Levantine impresario. The havoc wrought by this unprecedented cinema odalisque was incalculable. (1930)

Playing together like the meshed gears of a Rolls Royce, Dietrich and Gary Cooper gave the film what we call "pizzazz" and the French call *panache* under the mordant humor and exquisite sensibility of Sternberg's direction. (*Morocco*)

to push the donkey to one side of the road as the Legionnaires thud past—but not before the Colonel, marching at their head, gives the donkey a final push to get the animal out of the way, for the Arab didn't quite make it completely. And here, momentarily, the two opposing actions join (as in music two opposing rhythms finally cross and meet; a moment that gives the two their relation and the passage its meaning). It's a nuance, the smallest possible, but the scene is richer for it. Later in *Morocco*, during the famous scene of the engagement dinner of Amy Jolly (Dietrich) and LeBessière (Menjou), which begins gaily and suddenly starts to lose momentum and languish when the faint drum beats from the outside distance (this time laced with bugle flourishes) herald the approach of the Legionnaires returning from a skirmish with the Arabs, the single strand of action and sound (of the guests at the dinner party) becomes two strands at the moment when Dietrich, realizing her Legionnaire lover may be back, gets up in panic, breaking her necklace of pearls (her engagement gift from LeBessière), which she caught on the back of a chair in her haste (the rupture that suddenly makes of the one strand of the action two). She rushes out to join the column of troops outside, searching for her Legionnaire (Cooper), while back at the dinner party the conversation has slowed almost to a full stop and desperate but futile attempts are made to revive it. As the guests speak, LeBessière looks blankly at whomever is talking, but he hears nothing and, indeed, there is nothing to hear. The conversation is inane, turns on the weather, it is not worth hearing, ultimately it crumbles. All the life has gone out of the dinner party . . . just as years later Sternberg was to note in *Anatahan*, in his brooding commentary, that despite the violent fighting over the lone girl the shipwrecked sailors found on the island, when she left the island ". . . there was no more fighting . . . there was also no more life." The vital force of woman as the life-giver is one of the beautiful overtones of both films.

One could write a book on the subtleties of *Morocco* alone and its audio-visuals, which are as rich in their polyphonies as a score by Brahms or Ravel.

This kind of incandescent filmmaking, which illumines everything (in contrast to the present vogue for mystification and opaqueness), has naturally attracted no disciples. Most films today are apotheoses of the single-entendre, when they are not being "mystical" or "profound."

Literal expositions and redundancies have no place in Sternberg's art and those who say that *Anatahan* contradicts this have failed to feel the virtue of its simplicity. Here the "left hand," as in a piano score by Brahms or Ravel, for instance, is more important than the "right hand"—the former being, in this case, the eloquent commentary (mentioned earlier) spoken by the narrator, the latter being the images. Critics of *Anatahan* don't realize you could turn the images off and just listen to the sound track (or vice-versa, turn the sound track off and just watch the sequence of images) and the story of *Anatahan* would unfold itself with equal clarity. And, since both are so right for each other, they complement each other. The narrator of the commentary is supposed to be one of the survivors of this island incident and, indeed, there *was* one such who wrote a book about this from which Sternberg adapted his film. The book is written in the first person, as is the commentary. The technical fact that this method obviates the necessity for sub-titles to translate the Japanese dialogue seems to have been overlooked by its critics. They have curiously also overlooked the fact that the presence of Sternberg's voice is in itself a rare asset to the film, for he not only wrote the narration but speaks it himself. How many film records do we have of great directors' voices, in which we can study their personalties through their voices? Why are not *Anatahan's* critics grateful for this? Anyway, why must every film be made like every other film so that it is easily recognized as such and hence does not disturb but falls into a convenient category for the critic? Many critics were upset by the polyphonic *Mr. Arkadin*, but praised the decidedly nonpolyphonic *The Umbrellas of Cherbourg* (which leans with all its weight on one song by Michel Legrand) without apparently having even heard the wonderfully vertiginous music score by Paul Misraki in the former and being totally ignorant of the best of the *genre* of the sung-film, *Amphitryon*, by Reinhold Schuenzel and Franz Doelle, made in Germany in 1933. I am inclined to think that many film critics are tone-deaf or they would have remarked on the impeccably modulated timbre of Sternberg's voice uttering its glinting drops of sorrow, its evocations of eternal truths, which form the core of this remarkable outpouring of the human heart, which blends so beautifully in *Anatahan* with Ifukube's lovely music score. Besides being tone-deaf, I think many are blind, too. They look but they do not see. One of the most poetic moments in *Anatahan* has never to my knowledge been commented upon. It is possible it wasn't even understood. Several journalists asked me how the girl ever got off the island since this was never shown, they claimed. Keiko, the lone female on the island in *Anatahan*, is tired of being fought over and accepts the offer from an American warship waiting offshore to be returned to Japan, an offer made by leaflets dropped to all the shipwrecked Japanese sailors, an offer which they reject as an absurd enemy trick, not knowing the war is over and Japan was defeated. She stands on a promontory waving one of the leaflets to attract the attention of the ship while the narrator says, "A long time ago, Keiko said that if she had the wings of a bird she'd fly home." And at that moment her waving arms are like the flapping wings of a bird—and it is this motion which gets her off the island and back home. How simple and beautiful this is! But how unsensational! How invisible to the literal-minded. How unlike the palpable mystifications and symbolisms so portentously commented upon today. The corruption of the eye has never been more rampant. A distinguished psychiatrist told me the pseudo-Freudian symbolisms of 8½ were as phony as a three-dollar bill.

This brings us inexorably to the matter of sex, since Sternberg's work has been so often equated with eroticism, especially in his films with Dietrich.

Ironically, it is just here that Sternberg has been at his most discreet. In a medium that has become, as Edmond Greville put it, one in which "voyeurism and cinema are synonymous," the films of Sternberg are by comparison anti-erotic. The director's mind is so involved with the refinements of his technique that there is no impulse to wallow in erotic swamps. Like Stroheim and Pabst and all the great directors from Griffith and Chaplin to Renoir and Bresson, sex is implicit, not explicit in his films. Only once, and that only in a five-second shot, did he ever make an explicit erotic comment, in *The Blue Angel*, the brief shot following the first time we see Dietrich (on the stage of the cabaret).

She is singing "Ich bin die fesche Lola" and Sternberg cuts from a long shot to a medium close-up of her magnificent legs from the midriff down to accent not who is singing but *what* is singing. The shot is witty and laconically makes its point, after which it isn't necessary to belabor it.

After that, the director follows the dictum of Polonius, "by indirection find direction out," and proves that literalness in sex is not only unnecessary but ultimately inhibiting because a clever director can always imply more than a less imaginative director can show, with all his explicitness. (*Vide* the complete work of Lubitsch from *The Marriage Circle* to *Trouble in Paradise*.) Besides, literalness in sex is a redundancy, and redundancy is a bore. (*Vide* Bergman's *The Silence*.) There are no scabrous passages ever in Sternberg, not because he is a moralist—although he is that, in its most salutary sense, without any *a priori* moral judgments, like a psychologist or psychoanalyst—but because it would be a waste of film footage, every foot of which is precious to a director with so much to say, with so many comments to make. His characters hardly ever even kiss and on the rare occasions when they do it is usually hidden behind a fan, a cloak, a back, or in a half-light. He has better ways of indicating romantic feeling or, when he wants to, purely sexual ones, by innuendo in his incisive dialogue and telling imagery. So sure is he of what he is doing that he doesn't need to pander to his audiences. His is a cinematic language of the utmost circumspection. The salacious nature of so many of today's films results from their directors' inability to resist their own stimuli, their contempt for their audiences, or, at best (or is it worst?), the demands of their financial backers. Audiences flock to these pictures as to a trough. Catch-penny lubricity for the "vulgar herd" of Baudelaire . . . When Gauguin stated, "I wanted to make it possible for the artist to dare anything," he did not mean that the artist could even become a pornographer as long as he remained an artist. Such a thing is a contradiction in terms. Art, like morality, consists in knowing where to draw the line. Gauguin meant: to dare anything *stylistically*. There is not a single erotic canvas by him. There are erotic drawings by Utamaro, Beardsley, and Picasso, but it is not their best work. There are none, *mirabile dictu*, by Toulouse-Lautrec, for all the low-life of much of his subject matter. The really great artists don't succumb to their own stimuli ... at least not in their art.

Let us consider another criticism leveled against Sternberg in the past—his "mannerisms," i.e., his cinema calligraphy. Now, mannerism is a way of doing things and that is what style is. And if that style is different from the usual way of doing things it becomes a "mannerism." Such criticism is never leveled against directors without any recognizable style—thus, they have no mannerisms. Is this a good thing? All the great directors have had highly individual styles (and even certain lesser ones whose work has somewhat more than routine interest)—so they, too, have their mannerisms by this definition. Today, Godard and Antonioni may be said to have their mannerisms. Buñuel's shock-therapy via his surrealist inserts is a form of mannerism. Orson Welles, of course, is a striking example. In short, it is just those elements in their work that set them apart from others that could be (and often are) held against them. This kind of glib criticism, which appears on the surface to make sense but which actually makes no sense at all, is unfortunately epidemic in the cinema. Sternberg without his "mannerisms" would not be Sternberg, just as Stroheim without his and Griffith without his and Orson Welles and even Chaplin without theirs would not be what they are. Even if by mannerisms these critics mean "excesses" they are still wrong because they don't understand that even excess has its function in art, for through excess ultimate expressiveness is reached, ultimate statements are made. "Were it not for his excesses," said Romain Rolland, "Beethoven would not have been Beethoven." Art is not a cup of tisane or camomile tea, it is not polite for the sake of being polite, it is not a warm bath, it is not necessarily a comfortable or even a comforting experience. It is in constant ferment, it breaks barriers and defies accepted canons of conventions, it is by its very nature anarchistic, in the sense that Saint-Just was anarchistic. If Stroheim felt he needed 40 reels to properly present *Greed*, who understood better than he what he was talking about? When a conductor to whom Beethoven had presented a new score looked incredulously at it and said he (Beethoven) was crazy if he thought the violin section of the orchestra could play such a difficult work, Beethoven replied angrily, "What do I care about your lousy violins when the spirit moves me?"

Every artist of any distinction (distinction not only of merit but those characteristics which make him distinct from others) has his mannerisms. Dietrich and Garbo had theirs, Bardot with her monotone *moue* like a sulky Pekinese has hers, El Greco and Debussy had theirs, Maurice Chevalier and John Barrymore, Josephine Baker and Jascha Heifetz, Catherine Hessling, Paganini and Mistinguette, W. C. Fields and Picasso, Harpo Marx and Eisenstein, Frederick Lowe, the *douanier* Rousseau, Paul Klee, De Pachmann, Semmelweiss and Lenin, Brigitte Helm as the robot girl of *Metropolis*, Charles-Henri Alkan, *Hallelujah* and *Hallelujah the Hills*, Cocteau, Oscar Wilde, Harry Langdon, Norman McLaren, Satie . . . wherever you turn you find highly mannered artists, queer fish all. Their mannerisms are the stuff of their originality, to whatever degree, but even professional critics are not always capable of appreciating originality for what it is, and if they personally don't like it they call it a "mannerism" as if it were a tic. By and large, people don't want the *status quo* of their opinions and attitudes disturbed and have little capacity to make distinctions to the fullest degree, though they may make approximate distinctions. Pascal in his *Pensées* may have had this in mind when he said, "The greater intellect one has, the more originality one finds in men. Ordinary people find no difference between men." They may regard one film (since we are dealing with films) as better than another, but that the difference between the two may be that one is not just better but is as far above the other as the distance between the earth and the moon doesn't occur to them. Their horizon has not that wide a latitude.

There used to be a facetious axiom that everyone had two businesses, his own and the movies. Since the movies are a popular art, it is easy to give opinions on them and enlist solemn approval or equally solemn disapproval from others without necessarily anyone involved having any critical basis (i.e., an aesthetic formulated from the entire history of the films) for his opinions. This dilettantism spills over into much writing by professional film critics also. In no other art could a professional critic get away with as much ignorance about the art he is writing about than in that of the motion pictures. But in the comparatively short span of the cinema as an art, the 52 years from *The Birth of a Nation* till today, enough cogent and sober writing has taken place to have built up a solid basis for a real aesthetic from which students can learn, for the cinema is an art also to be studied, like any other, from books and other writings as well as from the works themselves. It is up to the teacher to guide the student through the maze of these writings, however, as more than in any other body of critical writing are there writings that obfuscate rather than clarify. Mis-statements of facts alone are particularly endemic to this field, being based on that old bawd, Dame Hearsay (so many films having disappeared or are not easily accessible), the repetition of facile shibboleths and half-truths, hoary canards that once made "good copy" and which die hard, lies told from ignorance and kept up for the royalties ... *Sic semper cinema!*

Mis-statements of evaluations are something else. Usually history rights these in time, *de gustibus non disputandum* notwithstanding, as it does where such mis-statements occur in the other arts. One need only accept the fact that there exist objective standards in all the arts by which their excellence is measured and that the works themselves fall into their rightful places apart from personal likes and dislikes (rationalizations of prejudices) as if governed by a higher power than the animadversions of critics, for far more harm has been done by not praising good work than by praising bad work. Thus, when Sternberg's first film, *The Salvation Hunters*, that highly poetic affirmation of life, was first screened, a Hollywood trade-paper of unlamented memory called *Harrison's Reports* said of it, "We cannot decide which of the two films, *Greed* or *The Salvation Hunters*, is the filthier piece of work. ... Thinking it over, we have decided that perhaps the more loathsome of the two is *The Salvation Hunters.*" It is obviously not enough just to have an opinion—beyond the "I-know-what-I-like" school of criticism, you have to be qualified to have an opinion. There goes your *de gustibus.* . . .

No, Sternberg's "mannerisms" do not exist in a vacuum and alone anymore than his art does. It is part of the whole clamorous and exultant world wherever interesting people are to be found in and out of the arts, in science and sociology too, wherever dedicated men and women with a salutary purpose are even "going against the grain" to accomplish their work.

Seen today, Sternberg's films remind us of all this, they are a reminder of the richness that has all but disappeared from the screens of the world, and of how beautiful it was to see the continuity of an intensely personal style maintained from film to film in a medium so frequently composed of anonymous works. Sex and violence are brazenly rampant on our liberated screens today but this liberation has only meant that those who exploit it have become slaves of their passions. Censorship at least enforced subtlety on the screen artist. Today you don't need to be subtle, you can be "frank," if that's the world for today's effusions. *Yesterday, Today, and Tomorrow* and *Night Games* have supplanted Lubitsch's *Kiss Me Again* and *So This Is Paris*. Is this really progress?

By richness I don't just mean striking pictorial composition but something even better—an attitude. At the end of a Sternberg film you know the director's attitude on a hundred things or more. Most modern films have no more attitude than a picture calendar (with someone's advertisement). They are impersonal works, carrying no personal statement. The picture is one thing—its director another; there is not necessarily any bond between them. That's never so in the work of a true artist. He makes a personal statement by everything, even the slightest and most casual thing, he does. Nothing happens by chance in such films—and that is their worth because everything in them has been inserted because it has value. This makes a rich film. It is also possible to become so mesmerized by the witchery of a Sternberg film that only when it is over (I'm thinking particularly of *The Docks of New York*) do you realize it has been a silent film. This also makes a rich film.

Best of all that make films rich are the human touches that make us smile inside before the smile is reflected on our faces or that tug even faintly at the heart in their brief passing, to remind us that we are still human beings for all our much vaunted cynicism in a cynical age and that it is an endearing thing to be in the presence of a work of art by another human being like ourselves, because it is sometimes possible to feel in the world that, in the final analysis, in the last reckoning, one is alone in those deepest recesses of the heart where it counts most. The brief shot of the tear-stained sleeping faces of the Sieppe children, after their spanking, on the bed during the wedding party in *Greed*; the Tahitian natives draped over the masts and rigging of the visiting schooner in the bay in *Tabu*, as if the boat had suddenly sprouted blossoms; after the saloon fight in *The Docks of New York*, when the husky stevedore (George Bancroft) accidentally breaks a chair over the head of one of his adversaries and, being sorry, lifts the man up and rubs his head like a mother would, "to make the ache go away," without even looking at him but surveying the havoc around him with faint amusement; Dietrich as the condemned spy in *Dishonored* taking the blindfold offered her by the young officer commanding the execution squad and with it wiping a tear away on the young man's cheek; the final shot of the humiliated Professor Rat in *The Blue Angel* back at his old school desk, the symbol of his former dignity as a man, grasping the desk with a grip of passion so strong that the nightwatchman who discovers him there cannot pry the dead man's hands loose from it—one of the all-time great moments of the cinema (not in Heinrich Mann's book but inserted by Sternberg); the *mea culpa* of the mother at the end of *An American Tragedy* when she knows her son will be executed; the basic fraternity of decency that should exist even among political or social antagonists that results in the rebel Chang's (in *Shanghai Express*) permitting the French officer to go freely, although his army passport says he was dishonorably discharged and he is illegally still wearing his army uniform, because he is visiting his sister and doesn't want her to know of his disgrace; Walter Huston's sudden realization of his defection as a father when he learns the truth about his daughter, Poppy, in *The Shanghai Gesture* and wryly remarks, "The sins of the fathers . . ." leaving the rest unspoken but completed in the hearts of the spectators; the return of the defeated Japanese soldiers, those who survived the war, back home, in *Anatahan*—selected by Sternberg from Japanese newsreel footage but so trenchantly chosen as to overwhelm the viewer; the marvelous ending of that same film with the return of the smiling survivors from the island on an airfield in Japan, then the unsmiling ghosts of those slain on the island over the girl—the background is a shadowy and amorphous wing of a huge plane on the airfield with the vague forms of a guard or two standing at attention as if in a dream—and finally the girl herself, watching the ghosts of those who did not return, as the narrator concludes, " . . . and if I know anything at all about Keiko, she, too, must have been there."

Once again, and for the last time, Sternberg has echoed the theme that has haunted all his films . . . that waste of life of which Rimbaud speaks in his *"Par delicatesse j'ai perdu ma vie . . ."*

Much is made of the film spectacle today—big sets, hordes of extras, astronomical budgets, all of which are milked to the *n*th degree until we are surfeited with just the idea of bigness for its own sake. But to film a fairly elaborate scene just for the sake of a nuance is far more spectacular and I ask you to recall one in *The Devil Is a Woman*: The morning after Concha has been beaten by Don Pasquale for tantalizing him, when she visits him out of pique. "I came to see if you had killed yourself, after last night," she pouts. "If you had really loved me, you would have killed yourself." She tastes his breakfast cocoa. "Terrible," she says. "I can make much better cocoa." He pays no attention to her, out on a balcony where he stands with his back to her. And while she chatters away the marvel occurs, for rising up from the early morning mist of the harbor below Don Pasquale's rooms are, barely discernible, the tops of the masts of sailing vessels tied up at the quai, gently swaying, bobbing slowly from side to side. Thus Sternberg evokes a small seaport on the Spanish coast (as deftly and as impressionistically as he evoked the fog-shrouded Mediterranean crossing in *Morocco*) and we can feel the cool morning air which contrasts so blessedly with the sultry events of the night before. And we are as grateful for it as Don Pasquale must be. It is one of the most ravishing shots in all cinema and yet it wasn't necessary, the scene would have played without it, but the fact that it was there enriched the scene and was yet another indication of that urge "beyond the call of duty" that is always a jubilant thing to see. The wedding feast in *The Scarlet Empress* with death also sitting at the table in the person of a skeleton who needs no invitation . . . This is the fourth dimension in filmmaking. *This* is spectacular filmmaking . . .

And finally—the audience . . .

What the late Hungarian composer Zoltan Kodaly said of music applies most acutely to the film also. "For most people," he said, "music is a kind of bath to wash in. They react with their nerves, not with their minds." Sometimes this reaction coincides with the work, more often it does not. A thing is to be fully understood, after all, only with the mind. Such cinema lapidary works as *Shanghai Express* and *The Devil Is a Woman*, done with the aloof reserve of a Degas and the all but numbing perfection of an Ingres, limned with that grave ecstasy a seventeenth-century Dutch painter could divine in painting the transparency of glass or the yellow curve of a lemon peel—how much of this color that Sternberg applied in his details, without revealing any sign of a "brush stroke" with his lens, did the audience see?

They looked for a *chahut* in his films, as they do in all films, and he gave them the formal cadences of a pavane.

. . .

There were no turd-kickers in his films, no false coyness, empty in the middle and leering at the edges. Neither were there fools in his films, for he confessed he encompassed all his characters, their weaknesses as well as their strengths. But he never had any truck with fools. As any artist does, he interpreted the world as he saw it, and like all true artists his was an integrity that was inauctionable.

What remains to be said? We could sum up his work by saying that the iridescent flame of his technique, unique in the cinema, has been put to the service of what the Slavs call *zoll* and the Germans, *Weltschmerz*, that world pain, that life-hurt, for it is a sad, guilty world, and his sad, misanthropic films reflect this. "All noble things are touched with melancholy," remarked Melville. There are few resolutions in his films, although there is sometimes a gallant sort of hope. Shall we say something before concluding about the man behind the artist? His fastidiousness, his intransigence, his implacability where his art is concerned? But that brings us to the artist again. Let us just say that those who truly know him would agree that the frost of knighthood is in his manner, this mandarin among Hollywood directors. There is a considerable name in the history of the cinema—Josef von Sternberg—and he has earned it.

Somewhere in the Old Testament is recounted the fable of the burning bush . . . something to the effect that "the bush burned and it was not consumed." It was a testament of faith in the glory of God, in Jehovah the beneficent. Good was the positive force on earth and evil the negative. The Judaeo-Christian religion has always needed miracles to impress its constituents, though that need does not militate in the least against its precepts, which are fine, if people would only practice them.

What is the history of art but a succession of fables? "Art is a lie which helps us to see the truth," said Picasso. "For the sake of truthfulness, one can even deny truth," said Goethe.

Art implies artifice, something artificial, but it also stems from the Latin, *ars* or *artis*, meaning skill in putting together. This is what the artist does in his creative imagination. "But he finds a way of return from his world of fantasy," said Freud, "back to reality. With his special gifts he molds his fantasies into new kinds of reality and men concede them a justification as valuable reflections of actual life."

Art is a constant miracle.

A personal note

Some reminiscences recalled from over the years . . .

We'd meet for lunch, which I welcomed, for it was then that he was at his most expansive, discussing the events of the day, a conversation invariably spiced with his acerbic wit. I had mentioned a light scandal currently peppering the gossip columns about an American heiress allegedly involved in an affair with her colored chauffeur, whom she was now suing for defamation of character or some such thing. A trial was in the offing. "Oh," he said, "she'll settle it out of court." "How do you know?" I asked. "Why should she go to court?" he replied, not missing a forkful in the steady rhythm of eating. "She'll say she didn't and he'll say she did."

As it turned out, it was settled out of court.

Shortly after that he departed for Japan to make *Anatahan*.

He came back like a real sailor with a duffle-bag containing a print of the film. It proved you could do everything with grace, especially if that quality was second-nature to you, as they say. He had a special white canvas duffle-bag constructed for him in Japan to contain the nine reels of the film, a handsome and jaunty thing drawn together with white rope, and it was certainly more sensible, since it made the print so much lighter to carry, than when encased in the conventional metal boxes.

Of course we talked over old times, such as when he informed Paramount that he wanted Adolphe Menjou for the third angle of the triangle in *Morocco*, the role of the suave LeBessière, and they objected. Menjou was through, finished, they said, a "has-been," in that sort of role, played by him principally in silent films under Chaplin, Lubitsch, d'Arrast, Mal St. Clair, and others. Sternberg insisted and had his way. "But I said to him (Menjou)," he told me, "before we began, that ideally I'd prefer to cast him as a shady

Levantine selling fake Turkish rugs from table to table on the terrace of a Paris café."

Menjou didn't exactly like that but he played well for Sternberg in *Morocco* and his stock rose considerably afterward, taking him out of obscurity into the second phase of his career, which was to last a long time. Just as *Morocco* rescued Gary Cooper from vapid Westerns and the movie equivalent of pulp-fiction and started him on a bright career almost equally as long. As for *Dietrich*, it made her—it was only afterwards that *The Blue Angel* was shown here. To make three careers in one picture is not only not bad it is spectacular. Add what it did for its director, himself, and you have a fourth.

He wasn't always as prescient as in the matter of the heiress and her chauffeur. In 1937 he was in London, just returned from a world tour. In an interview he stated this fact, adding, "I have talked to people high and low; there will be no war." Two years later, of course, World War II began.

Sometimes I would steer the conversation gingerly toward other directors. He liked Clouzot and René Clair, Chaplin, of course, and Stroheim's *Greed*. He couldn't stand Griffith. He liked Zoltan Korda's *Cry, the Beloved Country*. Eisenstein, with whom he was very friendly. Most of all, as I recall, he liked the work of Buñuel. Sternberg wasn't anymore superficial than was Oscar Wilde, both of whom were frequently thus labeled. (Wasn't it Eisenstein who said that if it hadn't been for his discovery of Karl Marx—Eisenstein had already discovered, that is, for himself, Leonardo da Vinci and Freud —he might have become "a cinema Oscar Wilde"?) Where Sternberg's own work was concerned, as well as the work of others, he was absolutely objective, despite all reports to the contrary. No one could sort the chaff from the wheat of his own films better than he, himself, could.

"Though my films have been, and still are, studied by other directors, here and abroad," he once said, "I regard them only as reasonably arrogant gestures of mine. They were often only protests against other films of the time.* Frequently they were attempts to investigate techniques

* Like Stravinsky's idea for a little travelling theatre, for which he composed his "L'Histoire du Soldat", as a protest against the orchestral mammothism of Mahler and Richard Strauss.

JOSEF VON STERNBERG 115

which might broaden their appeal. They don't carry my endorsement, they only carry my name."

Surely an apostolic utterance by a devoted disciple of Saint Cinema . . .

As I write these notes in the Spring of this year, I think of the note I recently sent him upon his return from Stockholm, where he attended yet another retrospective of his work. "I thought I was finished with the book," I wrote, "but they've asked for a personal note on you. Got any suggestions? It's not easy to do . . . I quake at the thought!" To which he replied laconically, "Don't quake."

So I'm on my own . . .

To him the highest callings are those of the creative artist and the dedicated teacher, though he has a healthy respect for science used to better the lot of man, which is to say, when it is not manifesting the destructive side of its schizophrenic nature.

He has taught film direction, e.g., film aesthetics ("since you cannot teach film direction—it requires an attitude"), at the University of Southern California and lectured at the University of California in Los Angeles. He has also lectured on this subject in many American universities and most recently at the hallowed Uppsala University and at the University of Lund in Sweden. This year he will also go to Sydney, Australia, at the invitation of the Sydney Film Festival, which this Spring had their own first retrospective showing of his films.

They say Kant never left Koenigsberg—but become a great film director and see the world. Or a great violinist, like Heifetz or Kreisler, both of whom Sternberg numbered among his many friends among the world's ornaments of the twentieth century.

Speaking of Kreisler, he had, of course, a broad Viennese accent straight out of the Wurstelprater, but not any broader than the Viennese accent of Sternberg when speaking German, thick enough so you could skate on it (it's slippery enough, heaven knows!) throughout the four seasons. I was present at a two-hour interview with the late Manfred Georg, editor of *Aufbau*, and not a word of English was exchanged between the two of them throughout the luncheon-interview. Sternberg's impeccable English, however, has not even the faintest trace of this Austrian accent and is, if anything, slightly clipped and Oxfordian, with an amusing admixture of pure Americanese. In Hamburg he addressed the large student body of a university in their own language.

But he is as circumspect in his speech as he is in his films. I have never heard him swear. Indeed, he is so meticulous not only in his writings but in his speech that sometimes he will disconcert his *vis-à-vis* (usually an interviewer, whose studied aplomb he likes to frustrate) by employing circumlocutions like "His name is not unknown to me" for "Yes, I know him." This usually stops you in your tracks. But you must hold on or you're lost beyond retrieving . . .

He is both a painter and sculptor, or at least he was, and several moody heads of Dietrich and a striking nude female torso (with an actual rosary draped around the neck) attest to this. He has himself been painted and sculpted (not to mention caricatured) all over the world and these portraits form part of the art collection (what's left of it, anyway, it once having been one of the most important private collections of modern art in America) that now adorns his home in Los Angeles. The rest is composed of books and more books, African and Oceanic masks, and exotic souvenirs of his many travels, interests, and, perhaps, fetishes.

Before that, he lived in a house he himself designed and had built on the Palisades overlooking the Hudson River in Weehawken. He carved the baroque wooden entrance door himself. The second floor consisted of one enormous room the size of the house itself with almost a floor to ceiling and wall to wall window so vast that it encompassed nearly the entire Manhattan skyline from the Battery to the George Washington Bridge. Talk about a room with a view! On the window ledge was nothing to obstruct the view, that is, nothing but a small figure of a saucy nude dancer looking out at the spectacular sight.

Several light wood-and-canvas director's chairs around a folding table served as a relaxed spot before the window where the gracious Mrs. Von Sternberg, as pretty as any of the heroines of his films, would serve drinks, liqueurs, or wild strawberries dusted with powdered sugar.

And before that, his "ivory tower" was a modernistic construction of steel, concrete, and glass surrounded by a foot-deep moat in which swam goldfish, a house also designed by him and set among the hills of San Fernando Valley, California.

Among the photos in his own collection I found one of him accoutered in ceremonial Korean robes (he even looked Korean with his then droopy, Charlie Chan moustache)—a souvenir of a temporary elevation to some Oriental deity by his idolators there.

Thirty years after sporting a trim Van Dyke beard in the Orient, behind which he embarked on the direction of *I, Claudius* in London on his return, he is sporting one anew, white this time, above which the ever youthful mischievous eyes still twinkle.

I played a record for him that I had run across once. It was called "A Hollywood Party" and consisted of parodies by the English night-club star, Florence Desmond, of various Hollywood celebrity guests at a birthday party given by Tallulah Bankhead. The guests included Zasu Pitts, Jimmy Durante, Garbo, and, *bien entendu*, Dietrich, who was riding the crest of the wave at that time, having just finished *Dishonored*, her third film with Sternberg. "I'm afraid I can't stay very long," the ebullient Miss Desmond has her say in a devastating voice imitation, low and somewhat breathless, "I have to be up at dawn to be shot—no, not another spy picture. Von Sternberg doesn't like me staying late at parties. When I tell him the truth, he doesn't believe me; when I tell him a lie, he does. So like a man. Goodbye!"

His only reaction to this was, "What people will do."

The English journalist Kevin Brownlow has reported the first meeting between Sternberg and Clive Brook, who was later to star in the director's *Underworld* and *Shanghai Express*. "I first met Jo when he was an assistant director on a picture in England," recalled Clive Brook. "He was Jo Sternberg then. On location in Wales, we slept in the same bedroom and I remember seeing him one morning staring into the mirror."

"Which is more horrible?" he asked. "With or without a moustache?"

"What do you want to look horrible for?" I asked.

"The only way to succeed," he said, "is to make people hate you. That way they remember you."

Some forty years later, Brownlow quotes Sternberg echoing that corrosive exchange with Clive Brook: "When I teach at universities on how to direct, I propose some absolutely horrible qualifications. I say a director must know languages, he must know the history of the theatre from the beginning of time. He must be an expert at psychoanalysis and must have some psychiatric training. He must know every emotion. And they say, 'Did you know all that?' And I say, 'No,' but then I never asked anyone how to become a director.'"

On another occasion, in 1954, he was invited to introduce *The Salvation Hunters* at a film society showing at The New School in New York, to which he had just returned after spending many months in Japan on *Anatahan*. He likes to accept as many invitations as he can, especially if they are from young people. But once on the podium, he began: "I don't know why I should introduce this film since I made it to introduce me . . ." Then he proceeded to tear it apart, noting only occasionally what was good in it.

A typical corrective, reflected in the filmography at the end of this book, is supplied by Sternberg in, say, the matter of Dietrich's costumes in her films with him, which played so important a part in delineating these roles. "Although ideas were sometimes submitted by the wardrobe people," he once wrote me, "I must say that everything essential was handled directly by me. I usually based the costume conceptions on some prior fantasies by painters and illustrators of long ago. . . . I do not wish to appear immodest but, with the exception of *Sergeant Madden*, *Jet Pilot*, and *Macao*, nothing in any of my films should be attributed to others save where I used the basic ideas of Hecht, Dreiser, Pierre Louys, Heinrich Mann, etc., to reorganize into my filmic conceptions. This is easily checked if you look at another director's handling of the same subject—say, *The Blue Angel* [the Edward Dmytrik remake with Mai Britt]. A director *writes* with his camera, whether or not it be his intention."

Apropos writing, Sternberg's handwriting might be described as "elegant rococo," with its small calligraphy punctuated by sweeping flourishes. He even had a typewriter whose type-face could also be described as "elegant rococo." At any rate, it was so elegant and so rococo that the publisher of his autobiography had to have the entire manuscript retyped so the typesetters could read it.

Today, between flying trips hither and yon, to this retrospective or that film festival, he lives serenely in California with Mrs. von Sternberg and their two handsome children, Nicky and Cathy.

"As I get older," he says, "I become more demanding of my own work. I have been busy with many things and I have not applied myself to the making of films. . . . Unless I can find a perfect vehicle, I will not direct another film. Another thing has interrupted my desire to make films. We live in a very disturbed world. I would like, if I make a film, not to disturb it more. I read a lot of literature, but I do not believe it is right for the screen. *The Blue Angel* was not based on the novel by Mann, it was merely stimulated by it. The motion picture is a unique art form and writers should write exclusively for it. So, while I am not working in the cinema, I take my car apart, play chess, study the evolution of the mail system in early China, and I also study anthropology and psychiatry . . . and somehow or other the time passes."

In a letter to me discussing *Anatahan*, sent from Japan, while still working on the film, he wrote, "I intend to set a standard of visual excellence with this picture." But he had crossed out the word "picture" and written above it "film." There is a difference. In that difference lies the history of the art of the motion pictures.

An Interview

In Nicole Vedrès's *Life Starts Tomorrow*, a film of interviews with notable men, the interviewer says to André Gide, "May I ask you an indiscreet question?" To which Gide replies, "There are no indiscreet questions, there are only indiscreet answers." It was enough to inhibit the interviewer from pursuing this course, not being the *bravo* that another interviewer was on a different occasion when the latter made so bold as to ask the great French writer, "Is it true, *cher maître*, that you are a homosexual?" To which Gide replied testily, with that refined distinction so characteristic of him, "No monsieur, I am *not* a homosexual, I am a pederast!"

Sternberg draws lines just as fine in his own interviews, while disconcerting his interviewers from behind his inscrutable Buddhalike mask, with what are often curt, acrid answers. He will sit, like the Grand High Lama, before his interviewer, speaking in a low, well-modulated and cultured voice, criticizing the questions when he finds them unworthy, or blunting what the interviewer might regard as a sharp question by answering it with such simplicity, with such forthrightness and directness in lieu of the "profound" or "epochally revelatory" statement the interviewer had expected, that the latter is nonplussed. In the ensuing havoc, his next question, in a desperate attempt to make up for his loss of ground (for it has already become a battle of wits, willy-nilly), is invariably sure to be both "safe" and, as a pitiful by-product of that "safety," asinine.

It is not that Sternberg doesn't like to be interviewed; he can be very voluble about his work when the questions are intelligently posed. It is just that he resents being put on trial, as if his interviewer was a self-appointed (as was usually the case) inquisitioner, and made to defend himself, i.e., his work, for no one would ever dare ask him any other kind of question. It is his work that matters, as far as the world outside him is concerned, and nothing else.

Interviews have been published (that's the amazing part of it) in verbal duels with him that were harrowing in the amount of "blood" they drew from the interviewer at the hands of Sternberg's sardonic rapier. They must be masochists to submit to such hazardous forays, but getting an interview from Sternberg at all is an heroic feat and a good journalist will not be intimidated by this "dragon."

What sets many of his interviewers on edge is that they feel they are in the presence of an egocentric celebrity. This unconsciously puts them on the defensive and in the course of the interview the process of transference takes place, all but invisibly, and suddenly an innocent question may, in the subtle change of ambiance, take on the tone of an impertinent one and the sparks start flying. The interviewer has unconsciously transferred his defensiveness to the subject of his "torment." And yet it is common for world celebrities to be egocentrics—a notable example in our time being Igor Stravinsky. And why shouldn't such men be? You will notice that mediocrities are never accused of that fault. But is it a fault? Not when thought out, for its basis is as it is used in philosophy, e.g., the world existing only as conceived in the individual mind. Great religious leaders, who certainly have never been accused of being egocentrics, have been directly or indirectly responsible for endless bloodletting in the cause of "holy wars" and other such genocidal massacres in the name of one god or another, but no artist, no matter how "egocentric" or "eccentric" or whatever, has ever harmed anyone. This goes for all artists in all fields and in all times. The real egocentrics, in the popular sense of the word, which occasioned these animadversions, are the villains of this world . . . from Holofernes to Hitler, and the like.

All of which is by way of lengthy introduction to the sample interview that follows, not one of the more harrowing ones, to be sure, but one of the gentler ones, so that it may be witnessed that the right questions fuse illuminating answers. For his usual prodigality of sarcastic energy when faced with stupid or banal questions, Sternberg here substitutes glints of his dry wit, such as his reply to the question, "When you directed *The Blue Angel,* were you conscious that you were transforming the actress you discovered into a myth?"

Sternberg: "I am always conscious when I direct."

Admittedly, it isn't much of a question because it should have been obvious to his for-the-most-part intelligent interviewers that Sternberg could then have had no idea of the plangent effect his star would have on the world in the context in which he put her. He knew what he was doing, but not that he was creating a *myth.*

Nor is his answer the *non sequitur* it appears to be because the question was a foolish one, spoken without thinking, to which he could not resist the facetious (but true) reply he gave. But it had the *wish* to be an intelligent question and this counts for something, too. Sternberg felt this and bypassed it gracefully and even with humor. Good will engenders good will.

—*Under whose influence were you at the time of* The Salvation Hunters?

—That's a difficult question. Everyone is influenced by his environment without realizing it. What has to be added in my case is that in the beginning I was influenced not by cinéastes but by writers and painters.

—*Your first film,* The Salvation Hunters, *could make one believe in the influence of Chaplin or even Griffith?*

—Only the titles are in the tone of Griffith. I detested Griffith's films. But I was bound to be influenced by Chaplin, whom I admired very much. I also admired *Greed* very much.

—*What is your judgment today of this first work?*

—*The Salvation Hunters* is not a good film but I couldn't prevent its showing as it belongs to the history of the cinema. First of all, we had many difficulties during the shooting. It is one of the least expensive films I know but the expenses were covered at the first showing. Then you must know that I did it as a reaction against the cinema of that era, in reaction mainly against stars and their gesticulations. The purposely slow action seems excessive to me now and I would do the opposite today. Finally, the meaning of the film seems naive to me. At that time I was young, which means terribly serious!

—*And now?*

—No longer at all!

—*Do you think that* Underworld *was your first important film?*

—I don't understand you. It is difficult for me to talk about my films, to say that this one or that one is better or worse. And above all, I don't think that any of my films are important.

—*You have just seen again* Docks of New York, *which is supposedly one of the last masterworks of the silent era. What was your impression?*

—It's the first time I saw this picture in a theatre since it was edited. Let me remind you of what I said before the showing: my first pictures seem stupid to me today, but stupidity is an ingredient of success. One has to be stupid to become a film director.

—*How did you react to the exploitation of the talkies?*

—There never were silent movies. The actors spoke and the titles reproduced their lines. There also was the accompanying music, which I preferred to choose myself. Thus, far from being opposed to the talkies, I made sound films myself right away. I even made one before *The Blue Angel.*

—*When you were directing this film, were you conscious of transforming the actress you had discovered into a myth?*

—When I'm directing I am always conscious. I don't work with my feelings but with my ideas, my brain.

—*Can you say a few words about* Shanghai Express?

—It is not a German film, as is sometimes stated, but an American one. I took great pleasure in recreating China in Hollywood, according to my imagination. Later on I went there. I took the Shanghai Express and it was quite different. This is why I'm glad I made this film before, following my fancy. I'm sort of a poet.

—*Certain historians and critics say that your work faltered during the later years. Do you think so too? For which reasons?*

—I stopped making films in 1935.

—*How do you explain this break-off?*

—My ideas about the cinema became more precise in the

light of my experiences. I was tired of seeing studio opposition to any creative ideas of the cinéaste at the different stages of its expression. Whereas a painter uses his brushes, canvas and colors, following only the bent of his imagination, the film director has to consider other men and human material.

After a trip around the world, I wanted to work according to certain principles; for instance, that we should be concerned to create expressive effects achieved in literature— and I hoped to work with more freedom. A lot of unhappy events prevented me from this, such as the tragic events of those years.

—*When you were shooting* Anatahan, *why did you choose to work in a studio in Japan?*

—Look at a map: Anatahan is an island located two thousand kilometers from Japan, halfway from the Philippines. Anyway, it was impossible to shoot a picture there: it's a jungle. But if I did not work on location, it was on purpose. I prefer to work in a studio. Outside, the tourists get in my way. I like to be comfortable; too bad if the actors are not. You have seen Docks of New York; well, that film was made in a studio. I recreated China in a studio for *Shanghai Express,* for *The Shanghai Gesture,* for *Macao.* . . . Everything is "artificial" in Anatahan, even the clouds are painted and the plane is a toy. This film is my own creation.

To reality, one should prefer the *illusion of reality.* Otherwise, you do what Jean Rouch did in *Jaguar,* which we just saw: you film everything that happens in front of the camera. This is documentary, it is not art.

—*Let us get to the more general questions. You seem to be disillusioned, disappointed in your career to such an extent that you minimize it. Still, you have known glory and your work is marked indelibly in the history of the cinema.*

—In 1930, as the result of a vote among professionals, I was named the American cinéaste whose influence had been the strongest. At that time, posters would advertise "Josef von Sternberg's new picture." It is my privilege to be dissatisfied with my films.

—*Did you not have a lasting influence upon certain cinéastes?*

—I cannot answer this question. I told you: it is very difficult to know by whom or what one is influenced. We are influenced by everything: these walls, this room ... A cinéaste may be influenced by a writer—Zola, for instance, in my case—or by a painter, as well as by another cinéaste. All these influences and all experiences combine themselves. Being influenced is nothing to blush about. Imitation is not embarrassing, as long as from this imitation one creates something personal. To imitate does not necessarily mean to copy.

—*Perhaps you suffered from not being able to express yourself freely?*

—I'm responsible for my films. I did what I wanted!

—*Not always! Will you say a few words about the troubles you had with the censors?*

—Little, in truth, with my finished films. *The Blue Angel,* for example, which they did not want to export, "as giving an unfavorable picture of Germany." On the other hand, there were films which I would have preferred not to be shown ...

—*Didn't you have to make personal concessions, sometimes, with regard to your plans? One gets the impression, when seeing certain of your films whose scripts are not on as high a level as the intentions, that you found it necessary to vulgarize your subjects for commercial reasons.*

—I don't understand what you mean when you speak of "the necessity to vulgarize my scripts for commercial reasons." As far as I know, I have never been vulgar.

—*It also seems that certain of your films have been "watered down" during the process of shooting or editing. Were you free in your work?*

—Of course there were certain limitations. For example, because of the actors. I had to compose with stars like Bancroft and Marlene Dietrich, so as to model their parts after themselves. I made seven films with Marlene Dietrich; in reality I wanted to make only two: *The Blue Angel* and *Morocco.* But she was bound by contract to a studio. In America, one can say that a cinéaste is free within the limits of commercial success.

—*Then you are concerned with the financial success of your films? What do you think of the audience?*

—One is bound to worry about the receipts but I don't

Dietrich sets a new pattern for the *femme fatale*. Here as an Austrian spy, X-27, trapping the traitor (Warner Oland)—the *milieu* is again World War I—in another "valse triste" by Sternberg to the memory of the last days of "alt Wien." (*Dishonored*—1931)

worry about the audience. What is the audience? How can you mingle the people of Tokyo, Berlin, Paris, and New York who will see the same film?

Whatever it is, in my eyes the public is stupid. The crowd is always stupid. Individually, men may have qualities; in a crowd they become stupid. I prefer to please myself.

—*Once more, you seem pessimistic ...*

—Why should I be pessimistic? *You* are the ones who think I am. Facing the same reality, two contrary reactions are possible: looking at a half-empty theater, the pessimist will say: "It's half empty," and the optimist: "It's half filled." I don't believe I'm a pessimist. Look at *Docks of New York*; it's an optimistic film.

—*You are supposed to have made the following disillusioned statement: "The cinema is an industry which could have been an art." Do you confirm it?*

—I don't think I said that. I don't think it's bad that the cinema is an industry.

—*But commercialism and industrial methods can obstruct and restrain personal expression.*

—There is nothing perfect in this world. It is normal for people to try to make money out of films. The problem of creation is an interior one.

—*But without money, a cinéaste cannot express himself, can he?*

—Sometimes it is preferable not to have money. Painters too—Van Gogh, Modigliani, Utrillo—worked in order to eat.

—*All they needed was a canvas and a few tubes of paint to create something. A cinéaste needs millions, which he receives only under certain conditions.*

—One must fight, fight, always fight!

—*You were nine years without making a film, from 1941 to 1950; and since Anatahan (1953) you have not made a single picture. One cannot interpret these long silences as simple failures of creativeness, can one?*

—I have mentioned to you all my difficulties—with producers, actors, distributors, managers, audiences. To me the important thing is to express myself as I can, as much as I can. Too many people have the power to deform and

A rare scene of a deglamorized Dietrich (with Lew Cody in *Dishonored*) in which she parodied a peasant wench with delicious humor, manipulated by the unerring strings held by the director.

mutilate our films. We wish there would be institutions to protect our creations, from their conceptions.

I tried progressively to secure more and more control of the animate and inanimate material through which I was to express myself. I wanted to *master* the cinema. Since 1924, for thirty-six years, I have been wanting to make my work easier, to change the conditions which gradually turned the cinema into this complicated machine, and to adapt it to creative work. It was a ticklish enterprise. I am sure that when I made a successful picture, its success was due only to stupid things. Film directors could do much better if they did not have to clash with futile absurdities and ignorance, and if they were *encouraged* by the financiers and the public.

—*A certain number of ideas, feelings, and themes reappear frequently in your films. Do you think your work has a general significance?*

—That's too broad a question. "It's not up to the chicken to speak about its own soup," the Russians say. I don't want to be enclosed in formulas. I like variety. I'm glad to have had an irregular career.

—*In several of your films, love triumphs over duty. Do you believe that love is the supreme value of life, the only one, perhaps?*

—"No, I don't believe that. Love is a driving element of life, but the supreme value to me is justice. Like for Zola!

—*You have, no doubt, a personal ideal?*

—I don't consider myself important in my own eyes. What is important to me is to behave like a human being, to know the joys of family life, and to educate people.

—*What has been your essential preoccupation as a cinéaste?*

—To find the means of expressiveness, to discover its possibilities. What interests me is expressiveness achieved by means of technical investigation.

—*Do you prepare your films minutely or do you believe in improvisation?*

—I love to improvise.

—*What do you think about the direction of actors?*

—Actors are material with which one works.

—*Which function do you assign to the décor?*

Again, as in the case of *The Wedding March*, Sternberg solves a problem for Paramount by filming *An American Tragedy* after the studio's rejection of Eisenstein's screen play. Phillips Holmes as Clyde Griffiths and Sylvia Sidney as Roberta Alden. (1931)

—I control the décor just as I control each element of the work I create.

—*Your films have a photographic style, homogeneous lighting. What importance do you give to lighting?*

—I am responsible for the lighting in my films. It is an element inseparable from photography.

—*You have made interesting experiments with color. Seeing* Jet Pilot *one gets the impression that your ideal would be to use color for personal, not realistic, ends. Do you think this purpose is still valid?*

—The ideal, indeed, is to use color in a personal and unreal way. I was limited in the total application of this principle for *Jet Pilot*, in which many scenes seem not to be my own.

—*You have kept a liking for symbols though they become more and more integrated into your films . . .*

—I have never deliberately introduced symbolism of any sort into my films though the composition of certain images one finds in them may appear as purposeful symbols to those who have decided to find one at every opportunity.

—*Have you edited all your films?*

—Yes, all of them. The changes were made later.

—*I will ask you another question which is too broad: what is your definition of the cinema?*

—That's a *very* broad and very difficult question. I would *like* to answer it because I have many ideas which I have never expressed. But I cannot do it in a few words; besides which, the translation could modify the meaning of my words. The next best thing is to refer you to my writings. I have published several texts on the cinema and I taught aesthetics of the cinema seven or eight years ago at the University of California.

The ideal is to experiment in films. I would especially like to study movement and sound. One cannot talk about the cinema with words alone. We are three persons here. Let one of us tell about a film he would like to make and the result will be three different films in our minds. We cannot understand each other in this way.

Finally, I must say that I am pliable and changeable. I don't know what I will think tomorrow.

—*What do you think succinctly today of the cinema's future?*

—It is unforeseeable. Oscar Wilde said: "What a pity that progress should go toward the future instead of going toward the past!"

—*Do you think that the cinema may still experience further decisive transformations such as sound, color, and wide-screen?*

—Why not? Anything is possible. And anything that is possible is worth trying. In my next film, I would like to try something new.

—*Do you believe, for instance, in the possibilities of the variable screen and polyvision?*

—Oh, yes, Abel Gance! Why not? It's the result that counts. If it works out, all the better!

—*Is television, in your opinion, a threat to the cinema?*

—Not at all. They are two completely different techniques. Television can do good things, but not the same things as the cinema.

—Recorded by Philippe Esnault and Michèle Firk and published in *Positif* (Paris) Nos. 37–38, January and March 1961.

Excerpts from Correspondence

The virtue of interviews is that they are—both questions and answers—spontaneous things. Letters, however, tend to be more studied and reflective. Both have their place in the task of presenting "the total man." So many interviews with Sternberg have appeared and he has been quoted so often that I decided to present, as personal statements by him on the art of the film in general and his own art in particular, completely new and unknown material. These half-dozen excerpts from letters, covering a span of 15 years from 1949 to 1964, present in highly concentrated form some of the attitudes that resulted in the films by him that we know.

To Curtis Harrington,
June 15, 1949

Poetry is not exclusive to any single medium of expression, and you will find a clue to much of my work, if not to all of it, in noting that I use images and sound like others have used words. It is difficult to take issue with a poet, except on the point of merit, since he is primarily concerned in ordering apparent chaos or, paradoxically enough, presenting chaos as an orderly phenomenon. I have always avoided emotionalizing my films, choosing rather to present emotion as a casual component of other elements. The world is avid for easily digestible formulas, and in exploiting film to carry no such apparent solutions, I could not escape severe criticism. But I also did not escape praise, though it was not always correctly applied. I only sought to find a way to sound out cinematic power, leaving it to others to employ it in selling emotions. Analyzing the laws of film is the job of a scientist who, too, must leave his emotions out of the result. At the core of science is the poetry of the universe—and ably or not I set out to investigate this, whenever I could do so without hurting others. The scientist is privileged to withhold his findings, not so the film director. Now I am not too sure that I always did this with full knowledge, but I am reasonably certain in the light of later developments that such were my drives and inclinations. I would like to close by encouraging you to pursue your studies in criticism and not be tempted to give reasons for the behavior of others solely because the questions have not yet been clearly articulated.

To Richard Griffith,
January 16, 1959

The artist who selects the size and shape of his canvas is usually influenced by what he intends to paint. But here, in our medium, where the artist as yet is as rare as a hen's square egg, the size and shape is predetermined. Gulliver pegged to the ground by the Lilliputians is just right for the present rectangular area, but Gulliver on his feet extinguishing the tiny Queen's palace fire by the most instantly available method becomes a problem. In my work I use the camera to include only that which the viewer is to see, and to exclude what is pictorial wasteland; I control the time of the visual impact and establish a tempo. That is no longer easy, there is now spiritual space on both sides, and the force, the flow, and the impulse is hampered by the spectre of a gaping void. But this is not the worst, the circular screen will come, the screen all around us will bring revolving chairs into use, the ceiling projection, currently in beautiful use at the Planetarium will compel us to lie down. But the ultimate hazard is not the shape of the screen, large or small, it is the audience that supports piffle and junk with enthusiasm. There will come all sorts of innovations to appeal to that audience, though ultimately, I wish I could foresee the joyous day when the text and the skill with which it is told will dominate this great art form.

You will recall that Oscar Wilde put it very nicely: "The only trouble with progress is that it goes forward and not backwards."

ON INFLUENCES

To W. G. Simpson,
December 26, 1959

On the general subject contained in your letter I would like to mention that there is little work on earth, if any, that is entirely without influence. Such influence is at times difficult to trace for it may be inspired by abstractions from an entirely unrelated field. Where influence is obvious it becomes imitation.

It is possible that some of my work has been imitated, as in many parts of the world I have been told that it has not been ignored. I have only seen one of Bergman's films, and that recently in Venice, and I perceived nothing that I could label an imitation of my work. I might add, rather lightly, that I do not think it too easy to imitate my work in films, as it might require so much skill in avoiding pitfalls, that such technical skill could more easily be applied to something less obvious. If, however, my work has served to subtly influence others in films or in any other territories, it would please me and not be contrary to my hopes. On the other hand I might add that I have had scenes taken from my work, or copied so bluntly, that this did not afford me any satisfaction, nor did such unimaginative use of the camera escape the disapproval of others who love the film as I do.

ON RESONANCE

To Rafael Bosch,
October 3, 1960

There is a Russian saying: "A chicken does not discuss its own broth," and it might help to explain my reluctance to indulge in articulating my ideas in any other medium than my chosen work. Much of what you said in your Caracas lecture may be pertinent, particularly the application of your quotation by Eisenstein. Amusingly enough, though Eisenstein wrote about horizontal and vertical montage, he never made use of it. I attempt to make my work completely homogeneous. Image, sound, abstraction, and the effect of these on the beholder are interlaced and must follow an inner rhythm and an orchestration which, though it vanishes with the film, remains as a *"Nachklang."* It is this "after-timbre," this ghost-resonance, this lasting vibration that I seek—though I may not achieve it. And it has no possible connection with whatever may be inherent in any German influence. I am not German, I was born in Vienna and came to the United States at the age of seven. This, I can assure you, is no clue to my work. Nor do I assume that you seek such clues. In your analysis you enter a labyrinth, the labyrinth of influences. That is not unambitious. For an observing and sensitive person it is almost impossible to escape the influence of even the most trivial experience, nor do I mean to infer that influence always comes from without. The human, being with his complicated heritage, is influenced in the main by as yet unlisted factors.

ON STYLE

To Tom Foral,
  May 2, 1962

Generally speaking, all art is an exploration of an unreal world. Style is the inevitable result of imposing control on the elements with which creative work concerns itself. It is not necessarily a confining of form, but it results from a search for abstraction not normally contained in presenting things as they are.

ON SURREALISM

To Yves Kovacs,
  May 25, 1964

Thanks for your letter of April 24 in which you ask me to comment on the subject of surrealism. I have been familiar with it since its modern beginning. I assume that you are not attempting to trace it back to Hieronymus Bosch and to those who influenced him. I have not been consciously influenced by this phase of the arts, though I must concede that nothing I have ever seen has not somehow been absorbed by me. As for direct influences on my work, this is dealt with at length in my book which is now being published. The title of my book is *A Guide to a Labyrinth*, which title might indicate to you the large scope of the questions that might be asked about all creative stimulants.*

* Although this book, when published the following year, was titled *Fun in a Chinese Laundry*, no change in the text was made to "fit" the new title, save for a fleeting reference to it.

Extracts from Scenarios

SHANGHAI EXPRESS
Opening Sequence

The following is from the preliminary script as written by Sternberg. As he edited the film himself, eliminating certain scenes and details, modifying others during the actual shooting, frequently adding different details (like the sudden startling close-up of a recumbent camel attended by a coolie, seen against the huge glistening wheels of the train getting under way, which was not in the original script), the released version of the film was often different. The determining factor of the ultimate visuals and sound track were the nuances sought by the director to give the work a "symphonic curve," as a composer orchestrates a score. When a director exercises the fullest autonomy over his work, as Sternberg did, he becomes both conductor and composer. The result is an authoritative performance of an original work.

FADE IN:

EXTERIOR: PEKING CITY CANAL—DAY—
CLOSE SHOT—

of a dozen half-naked coolies running abreast on native treadmill which pumps water into a large pipe.

DISSOLVE TO:

FOLLOW SHOT—

of pipe to show destination of water. The pipe rises on supports which overhang railroad track and tender of the great American engine of the Shanghai Express, the side of which should be marked with the proper Chinese characters.

DISSOLVE TO:
FULL SHOT—

of coolie cleaning window of second-class coach. Information board fastened to car beside window reads down:

Peking,

Tientsin, Tsinan,

Yenchow, Sutsien,

Chinkiang, Pukow,

Shanghai.

As window-cleaner rubs window we see faces of Chinese passengers gradually appearing behind cleaned glass.

DISSOLVE TO:
ANOTHER FOLLOW SHOT—

of train, showing a gang of coolies loading baggage into baggage car; another gang loading sacks of mail and express into next car; while still another gang is filling storage tanks of dining car with ice and provisions. We pass an armored car in front of which a Chinese officer is inspecting a company of soldiers which is to guard the train on its journey to Shanghai.

DISSOLVE TO:

FULL SHOT—

of station filled with Chinese pedestrians and European stragglers. A native produce market is in operation on station platform. A company of Chinese soldiers, carrying rifles, is waiting for its train to embark.

EXTERIOR AND INTERIOR: PEKING RAILROAD STATION—FOLLOW SHOT—

of large poster on wall of station advertising in Chinese and English that the Shanghai Express is the fastest train-de-luxe in China and showing its route from Peking to Shanghai, etc. In foreground we see a small crowd surrounding public water-heater, drawing hot water to make tea. All races are represented—Chinese, Manchus, Tartars, Russians, Mongolian lamas, and the air is filled with the racket of a dozen tongues. CAMERA GOES INTO STATION and shows Mrs. Haggerty, a boarding-house keeper, entering from the street door. She carries a small grip in one hand and in the other she carries a large closed lunch-basket. She is breathless with haste and goes to ticket window. She carefully sets down basket and addresses the ticket agent, who is an elderly Englishman.

MRS. HAGGERTY (in Cockney dialect and all in one breath): *The Shanghai Express ain't gone yet, has it? I wants a ticket to Shanghai—first-class, please.*

Rev. Carmichael, carrying a grip, has entered behind her and is waiting his turn with more or less impatience. At the next window a long queue of Chinese farmers and coolies are waiting to purchase second-class and third-class tickets.

TICKET AGENT (answering Mrs. Haggerty with a precise, cultured accent): *Thirty-five dollars and twenty-five cents Mex, Madame.*
MRS. HAGGERTY (counting out money): *Is there a dining car this time?*

Rev. Carmichael listens with increasing impatience and indignantly consults his watch.

TICKET AGENT (briskly—as he takes money): *Yes, Madame—everything but a Turkish bath!* (Then giving her ticket in exchange.) *Here you are—*
MRS. HAGGERTY (giving him a card): *I keeps a boarding-house in Shanghai—and very respectable it is—Yorkshire pudding a specialty—and if you're ever down that way—*

The rest is drowned out by an angry snort of impatience from Rev. Carmichael. Mrs. Haggerty, startled, backs away from the ticket window, gives Rev. Carmichael an indignant sniff as she picks up grip and lunch-basket and exits toward train.

MOVING SHOT—

of Mrs. Haggerty as she goes to gate of ticket inspector, a young Englishman. She gives him her ticket and as he punches it he glances at lunch-basket she is carrying.

TICKET INSPECTOR: *What's in that basket?*
MRS. HAGGERTY: *Just a little snack of lunch my niece put up for me—*
TICKET INSPECTOR (sharply): *No animals?*
MRS. HAGGERTY (haughtily): I hopes not!

She steps back as four coolies enter carrying a luxurious curtained palanquin. The jeweled hand of a Chinese woman is extended through curtains. The long-nailed fingers are holding railroad ticket. Ticket Inspector takes it, pushes aside curtains, glances at occupant, nods recognition, punches ticket, and hands it back to owner. Hand disappears inside curtains and coolies carry palanquin out toward train, followed by CAMERA.

EXTERIOR: PEKING STATION—MOVING SHOT—

of coolies as they carry palanquin through throng jabbering in tongues of all nations to track where Shanghai Express is waiting. It passes observation car, third-class and second-class car, decorated with proper Chinese characters, jammed with coolies and farmers who are leaning out sides, saying goodbye to relatives and friends, buying food from hucksters, chatting with a group of soldiers. The palanquin pauses in front of open doorway of first-class car.

Sam Salt, the bookmaker, is standing here comparing watches with the British Station Master. He glances at palanquin as curtains are drawn aside and Hui Fei, a Chinese courtesan, gets out. She speaks in Chinese to coolies, who take baggage out of palanquin and follow her as she exits into train. Sam Salt, turning a sage and wordly eye on the Station Master, resumes serious business of setting watch.

SAM SALT: *Twelve forty-three—you say?*
STATION MASTER (putting his watch away): *Exactly.*
SAM SALT: *How soon do we leave?*
STATION MASTER: *On time—in seven minutes—*
SAM SALT (with a grin): *It'll be the first train in China that ever left on time!* (He snaps a card out of his vest pocket and hands it to Station Master, adding affably.) *I run a little book down Shanghai way, and if you ever want to lay a bet on anything that's going anywhere—barring twins and foot races—just drop me a line—Sam Salt's the name—*
STATION MASTER: *Thanks.*

Dispatcher's clerk has entered with sheaf of train orders. He gives them to Station Master, who takes them, nods to Sam Salt and starts up toward engine, glancing at orders. CAMERA, following him, shows groups of people saying goodbye to passengers leaning out doorways and windows of armored first-class cars.

Chinese officer of train guard chatting with native girl who leans out window. His soldiers standing at ease. Car inspectors testing the air brakes and tapping wheels. Coolies still loading ice and provisions into dining car—mail and express and baggage in other cars speeding up to the last-minute rush. Station Master pauses by engine, where a Chinese conductor is chatting with a Chinese engineer. He hands each a copy of orders, saying:

Here you are, lads—all clear till you meet No. 2 *outside Tientsin—*

DISSOLVE TO:

INTERIOR: PEKING RAILROAD STATION—FULL SHOT—

of Rolls limousine stopping outside street door. A young

woman, wearing a heavy dark veil, alights and comes into station, followed by Chinese chauffeur, who carries her hand baggage. CAMERA follows her as she goes with quiet certainty across station to gate of ticket inspector, who is just punching ticket of Henry Chang, an Eurasian merchant. Latter is glancing at headline of newspaper—*The North China Star*. (NOTE: Please get copies of Anglo-Chinese newspapers.)

The young woman produces her ticket and Chang, taking his ticket from inspector, looks her over with an eager, appraising eye, gazing at Lily over his shoulder with increasing interest as he starts off toward train, followed by CAMERA.

EXTERIOR: PEKING RAILROAD STATION—
MOVING SHOT—

of Chang as he walks out toward train. He is furtively accosted by a shabby young Chinaman who has evidently been on the lookout for Chang. Latter does not stop and young Chinaman, walking at his side, speaks rapidly in Chinese to Chang, who meanwhile is looking around to see if they are being observed. Then, making a curt, silencing gesture, Chang walks on, allowing the young Chinaman to drop behind. He pauses by platform of second-class coach, looking after Chang, who is encountering the Station Master, a weather-beaten Britisher in a neat uniform, who greets him with a smile of recognition and strolls along train with Chang.

(As he does this.) *Glad to have you with us again, Mr. Chang—you haven't patronized us for several months—*

Chang nods, looking back over his shoulder in Lily's direction, while the Station Master, walking along train with him, continues without pause.

—I suppose you've been concerned about the rebellion— but there's really nothing to worry about—the Shanghai Express always gets through on time—

At this moment a window in first-class car is jerked open and Rev. Carmichael sticks out his head.

CARMICHAEL (angrily): *Guard!*
GUARD (entering and touching cap): *Yes, sir?*
CARMICHAEL: *Come in here—*

Guard obeys and exits into car, followed by CAMERA.

INTERIOR: VESTIBULE ARMORED CAR—
FOLLOW SHOT—

of guard going to door of compartment where Rev. Carmichael stands beside small pile of luggage. Inside we see Hui Fei, the Chinese courtesan, smoking and playing solitaire.

(To guard.) *I won't share a compartment with this woman!*
GUARD: *Change tonight.*
CARMICHAEL (angrily): *You'll change me now! I haven't lived in this country ten years not to know a woman like that when I see one!*

Hui Fei looks up at him—then resumes game. Guard picks up his bags as another guard enters with luggage belonging to Shanghai Lily. She follows guard, who exchanges short conversation in Chinese with other guard. Result is that Lily is given share in Hui Fei's compartment while Rev. Carmichael is led away to more respectable precincts. As he goes he says to Lily:

CARMICHAEL: *You may not find this compartment entirely to your liking—*

He glances significantly at Hui Fei. Lily's glance follows his. She comprehends Hui Fei's profession.

LILY: *Why not?*

Hui Fei looks up at them—and then goes on with her

game. Lily jerks off hat and veil, throws it up into rack and motions guard to put bags under the seat. Rev. Carmichael, staring at her, says half-apologetically:

CARMICHAEL: *I didn't mean to offend.*
LILY (glancing at Hui Fei): *Probably not—me.*

With that rebuff Rev. Carmichael makes his exit, following guard down vestibule to door of another compartment. Chang has been an interested spectator of this scene, and smiles at Hui Fei, who glances at him, rises, and closes the door.

INTERIOR: MRS. HAGGERTY'S COMPARTMENT —FULL SHOT—

of guard opening door and depositing Rev. Carmichael's luggage on floor of empty compartment which also shows signs of occupancy. He exits and Rev. Carmichael enters, staring suspiciously at Mrs. Haggerty's grip, which rests on best seat, and lunch-basket, which has been shoved under other seat.

EXTERIOR: ARMORED CAR—STATION PLATFORM—FULL SHOT—

of Mrs. Haggerty leaning out vestibule window and buying *Saturday Evening Post* from Chinese huckster.

MRS. HAGGERTY (looking at magazine): *Here—wait a bit —this says August 15th—1927—*
HUCKSTER: *Latest number, Madame.*
MRS. HAGGERTY: *But I tell you it's four years old—*
HUCKSTER: *Latest number, Madame.*

Mrs. Haggerty turns helplessly to Colonel Lenard, a grizzled old French veteran who is leaning out adjoining window.

MRS. HAGGERTY: *Is this 1931 or am I out of me mind?*
LENARD (with a polite smile—in broken English): *Madame,*

*I'm sorry, but I don't speak English enough to answer you
—je ne parle pas anglais, parlez-vous—français?*

FULL SHOT—

of Captain Harvey, a British army officer, leaning out window of compartment and chatting with a fellow officer who stands on platform. Latter is joined by a young subaltern who has been roaming along train.

SUBALTERN (to Captain Harvey): *I say, Harvey, you're in
for a good time! D'you know who's on this train?*
HARVEY: *Who?*
SUBALTERN: *Shanghai Lily!*
HARVEY: *Who's Shanghai Lily?*
OTHER BRITISH OFFICER: *Don't tell me you haven't
heard of Shanghai Lily! Everybody in China knows her!
She's a notorious Coaster—*
HARVEY (puzzled): *What in the name of Confucius is a
Coaster?*
SUBALTERN: *You're hopeless, sir! A Coaster's a woman who
lives by her wits along the China Coast—*
HARVEY (drily): *I dare say I shan't be able to avoid her—
on a three-day journey—*

INTERIOR: HARVEY'S COMPARTMENT—FULL
SHOT—

of guard entering with heavy load of hand-baggage belonging to Eric Baum, a German invalid. Latter follows guard into compartment, muffled up in a heavy overcoat, with a coolie bringing up rear with another load of hand-baggage. Baum, opening a heavy grip, which contains about fifty pounds of Chinese cash, takes out a string, gives coolie and guard the proper tip, and as they exit Baum goes over and gently taps Captain Harvey, who is leaning out window, on the arm.

BAUM (in German—as Captain Harvey draws in his head):
*Sir, I am an invalid, and it is very dangerous for me to
travel in a compartment where the window is open—*
HARVEY: *Sorry—*(Then, closing window, he starts toward

door, asking Baum in a sympathetic tone.) *Anything I can
do for you?*
BAUM (in broken English): *I can look after myself, thank
you—*

He sneezes violently and glares at open door, which Captain
Harvey hastily closes behind him. Baum, buttoning up his
overcoat, proceeds to make himself comfortable, removing a
small bag, which belongs to the other occupant (Colonel
Lenard) from the best seat and covering his knees with a
rug. Then door is slid back and Colonel Lenard enters.

LENARD (in French): *Whew! It's hot in here! D'you mind
if I—?* (He starts to open window, but Baum stops him
with a gesture of formal protest.)
BAUM (beginning in German): Sir, I am an invalid—

CUT TO:

INTERIOR: MRS. HAGGERTY'S COMPARTMENT
—FULL SHOT—

of Rev. Carmichael stretched out in best seat reading a
book. Mrs. Haggerty enters and sees him. He looks up at
her, realizes she is owner of luggage in other seat and rises
with a snort of disgust.

MRS. HAGGERTY (coquettishly): *You don't mind?*
CARMICHAEL (angrily gathering up his things): *It just
means I'll have to move again!*
MRS. HAGGERTY (in surprise): *Why?*
CARMICHAEL (disdaining to explain, sticks head out win-
dow): *Guard!*
GUARD (entering outside): *Yes, sir?*
CARMICHAEL: *Put me in another compartment—and if
there's anybody in it—be sure it's a man!*
GUARD (outside): *Yes, sir—*

He exists and Rev. Carmichael pulls in his head.

CLOSEUP—

of lunch-basket under seat. Top is open and Mrs. Haggerty's dog (which she has concealed in lunch-basket so she could smuggle her pet aboard train) sticks out head and is stepped on by Carmichael. Dogs lets out a yelp of pain.

FULL SHOT—

of Rev. Carmichael uttering an exclamation of alarm. He jumps away and looks down under seat.

CARMICHAEL (seeing dog): *What's that animal doing in here?*

MRS. HAGGERTY (in alarm—as guard enters outside in vestibule): *In Heaven's name—hush—they'll take him away from me—*

GUARD (entering and seeing dog): *No dogs allowed—*(He picks up dog by scruff of neck and starts out, saying.)— *belong in baggage car—*

MRS. HAGGERTY (following him in alarm): *He won't do harm—let me have him—*

INTERIOR: VESTIBULE ARMORED CAR—FOL-LOW SHOT—

of guard making off with dog with Mrs. Haggerty following him in alarm.

EXTERIOR: TRAIN—STATION PLATFORM—FOL-LOW SHOT—

of guard alighting with dog and starting up toward baggage car with Mrs. Haggerty threatening at his heels.

I'll have the law on you—if you harm a single bone in his head—he's got to have his biscuit twice a day—and nothing but boiled water—

CONDUCTOR'S VOICE: *All aboard!*

Mrs. Haggerty hears the cry taken up along the train.

She stops, torn between conflicting emotions. There is a

chorus of shouts and last goodbyes. Mrs. Haggerty yells after dog.

MRS. HAGGERTY: *Don't worry, Waffles—I'll look after you*—(Then she turns and runs back toward car.)
VOICES OF TRAINMEN: *All aboard!*

CLOSEUP—STATION CLOCK

It is exactly one o'clock.

INTERIOR: PEKING RAILROAD STATION—CLOSE SHOT—

of British ticket-seller pulling down window and shade.

FULL SHOT—

of ticket inspector closing and locking gate.

EXTERIOR: ENGINE SHANGHAI EXPRESS—CLOSE SHOT—

of bell starting to ring.

CLOSE SHOT—

of native engineer in cab of engine. He is looking back along train for signal to start.

CLOSE SHOT—

of native conductor waiting for coolies to toss last sack into mail car. He turns and makes hand-signal out of scene as coolies exit with empty truck.

CLOSE SHOT—

of engineer answering with a toot-toot of whistle and slowly pulling open throttle.

CLOSE SHOT ENGINE WHEEL

of giant piston as it starts to move and great jet of steam escapes with a hissing roar.

FOLLOW SHOT—

along train as it starts, with conductor and brakeman climbing aboard and guards closing doors.

INTERIOR: CHANG'S COMPARTMENT—MOVING TRAIN—FULL SHOT—

of Henry Chang, the Eurasian merchant, and Sam Salt, the Shanghai bookmaker, occupying opposite seats.

CHANG (glancing at his watch): Well, we're off on time—
SAM SALT (with an air of delicate approach): *Say, partner, d'you ever make a little bet? My name's Sam Salt*—(Snapping out a card and handing it to Chang.)—*I bet on everything under the sun going right or wrong—take your choice —and I'm willing to give you odds that this old rattler doesn't get into Shanghai on time!*
CHANG (with a queer, unfathomable smile): *Sir, let me remind you that China is in the throes of a civil war—and we'll be fortunate to arrive in Shanghai at all*—

Then door slides back and guard enters with Rev. Carmichael. Guard sullenly dumps bags on floor and exits. Rev. Carmichael, looking over his fellow-passengers as they do the same to him, puts his bags up in rack and fussily brushes off seat. Sam Salt turns his worldly eye on Henry Chang. Rev. Carmichael sits down, covertly surveying his companions with an air of grouchy contempt.

EXTERIOR: PEKING STREET—FULL SHOT—

of Shanghai Express slowly puffing down middle of busy Chinese street decorated with banners and dragons. We have left modern China behind at railroad station and are entering a China that is age-old. The street is teeming with ancient traffic. Woman bargaining with shopkeepers. Hucksters crying their wares. Shopkeepers and patrons coming out to watch train pass. Two coolies darting by with a sick man in a hammock.

Farmer staggering by with a crate of chickens. Mothers running out and screaming at children to get off track. Engine approaches, slowly gathering headway. Two coolies carrying a squealing pig in a sling dart across track ahead of engine. Engineer waves to Chinese girl in window above shop. Her father comes out and curses engineer. Latter grins and gives him a toot from whistle. Shopkeeper runs into shop and comes out wearing dragon's head and screaming fresh curses, shaking his fist after Shanghai Express as it slowly pulls by down street—soldiers and passengers sticking heads out of windows of coaches. Engine whistle suddenly begins to blow a frantic warning.

FULL SHOT—

of cow nursing calf in middle of track. Engine enters with screaming whistle and brakes. Stops ten feet away from cow, which calmly continues to chew cud. Trainmen alight from train and run forward. Crowd swiftly gathers. Owner of cow excitedly enters. Trainmen bawl him out in Chinese as he removes cow and calf. Owner and crowd bawl out trainmen. Brakeman motions them back and raises flag to signal engineer to go ahead. He pauses as he sees a Chinese funeral procession starting across track.

FOLLOW SHOT—

along train as passengers lean curiously out of windows to see cause of delay. Hucksters come up, crying their wares. Coming to first-class car, we see Sam Salt looking out of vestibule window.

SAM SALT (as camera passes him): *Even money we don't get away for an hour!*

CARMICHAEL (sticking out head): *What's wrong now?* (He turns to Henry Chang, who is looking out next window.)

CHANG (sarcastically): *You're in China now, sir—where time and life have no value—*

The "Dreiser breather" has done Sternberg good. He returns to Dietrich more the cinema Ingres than ever with *Shanghai Express*—the most famous train journey in screen annals—in a film of the purest lambency. Clive Brook and Dietrich. (1932)

CAMERA PASSES ON to Captain Harvey, who is leaning out of adjoining window. Shot should include Lily, who is looking out of window behind him. Harvey turns and sees Lily in adjoining window. She glances at him. They slowly recognize each other.

HARVEY (in amazement): *Magdalen!*
LILY (with a smile): *Well, Doctor—I haven't seen you in a long time—*

They study each other intently for a moment, both smiling. Finally Lily says:

You haven't changed a bit, Doctor—maybe a little grayer —that's all—

HARVEY: *You've changed a lot, Magdalen—*
LILY: *Have I, Doc? D'you mind me calling you Doc? Or must I be more respectful?*
HARVEY (smiling): *No. You never were respectful. And you always called me Doc.*

Lily looks at him with a faint smile, half-affectionate, half-reminiscent.

There is a toot-toot from the engine, the sigh of released air-brakes, and train starts with a jerk.

FOLLOW SHOT—

of Lily and Captain Harvey turning away from window. He goes with her to door of her compartment. The past has reached out and subtly touched them. The years have rolled up like smoke. They are looking at each other— both deeply stirred.

I didn't think I'd ever run into you again, Magdalen—
LILY: *Have you thought of me much, Doc?*
HARVEY: *How long has it been?*
LILY: *Five years—almost.*
HARVEY: *Well, for five years I've thought of nothing else, Magdalen.*

First-class compartment from Pekin to Shanghai on the Shanghai
Express and two of its assorted passengers, Hui Fei (Anna May
Wong) and the "notorious coaster," Shanghai Lily (Marlene Dietrich).

LILY (smiling): *You were always polite, Doc. You haven't changed at all.*

HARVEY (after a moment): *You have, Magdalen—you've changed a lot.*

LILY (in mock alarm): *Have I lost my looks?*

HARVEY (soberly): *No—you're more beautiful than ever.*

LILY (puzzled): *Well, how have I changed?*

HARVEY: *I don't know—I wish I could describe it—*

LILY: *Well, Doc, I've changed my name.*

HARVEY: *Married?*

LILY (shaking her head): *No! It took more than one man to change my name to Shanghai Lily—*

HARVEY (staring at her): *Shanghai Lily?*

LILY (smiling): *Yes—the white flower of China—you've heard of me—and you've always believed what you've heard—*

HARVEY (smiling): *I still do.*

She shrugs and opens door of compartment. Hui Fei sits at table still smoking and playing solitaire. She glances up at them—then goes on with her game. Captain Harvey, constricted by the presence of the Chinese woman, looks at Lily in silence for a moment. Rev. Carmichael, passing by in vestibule, gives them both a curious stare over his shoulder as he exits.

Well, it was nice to see you again, Magdalen—
LILY (looking at him): *Oh, I don't know—*

She turns to chair upon which is case containing Victrola. She opens case, puts on record, and touches lever. There is a noisy blare of musc and song as Lily lifts her eyes at Captain Harvey.

INTERIOR: MRS. HAGGERTY'S COMPARTMENT—
FULL SHOT—

of Mrs. Haggerty hearing music in adjoining compartment. She brightens up, rises, and exits into vestibule.

INTERIOR: LILY'S COMPARTMENT—FULL
SHOT—

of Lily and Captain Harvey looking at each other in silence while Victrola plays record. Mrs. Haggerty, entering in vestibule, smiles at Captain Harvey and sticks her head into compartment, nodding affably to Lily and Hui Fei.

MRS. HAGGERTY: *I heard your gramophone, ladies—and thought I'd come in and get acquainted—if you don't mind?*
LILY (welcoming the interruption): *Not at all—come in—*

Mrs. Haggerty flutters in and sits down. Captain Harvey starts to go.

MRS. HAGGERTY (calling to him in coquettish alarm): *I'm not driving you away, I hope?*
HARVEY (politely—as he exits): *Oh, no—*

Lily, winding up Victrola, looks after him. Hui Fei looks up at Lily—and continues to regard her, lighting another cigarette.

MRS. HAGGERTY (with her best social air): *It's a bit lonely on a train, isn't it? I'm used to having people around. They put my dog in the baggage car—that's why I dropped in on you—*

Lily smiles. Hui Fei, without looking up—laughs softly. Mrs. Haggerty, feeling the ice is broken, chatters on

I been visiting my niece in Peking—she married a seafaring man—he hasn't been home in four years—and she ain't been very cheerful—I has a boarding-house in Shanghai—Yorkshire pudding's my specialty—and I only take the most respectable people—(She hands out cards to Lily and Hui Fei.)

LILY (as she looks at card): *Don't you find respectable people terribly dull?*
MRS. HAGGERTY (startled out of her wits): *You're joking, ain't you? I've only known the most respectable people— you see, I keep a boarding-house—*

LILY (puzzled): *What kind of a house did you say?*
MRS. HAGGERTY (icily): *A boarding-house!*
LILY (thus enlightened): *Oh!*

She laughs in great amusement, and Mrs. Haggerty haughtily turns her back on her.

MRS. HAGGERTY (ingratiatingly to Hui Fei): *I'm sure you're very respectable, Madame*—(But her rising inflection indicates a faint doubt.)
HUI FEI (smiling—and in good English): *I'm sure I don't quite know the standard of respectability that you demand in your boarding-house, Mrs. Haggerty*—
MRS. HAGGERTY (suspicious of Chinese humor): *I'm afraid I've made a terrible mistake*—(Haughtily rising and starting toward door.)—*I better look after me dog!*

She goes to door. As she exits into vestibule, native guard enters with hatful of telegrams. He speaks to Hui Fei in Chinese and gives her a telegram.

LILY (to guard—as Hui Fei eagerly opens telegram): *Nothing for me?*

Guard looks through telegrams, shakes head, and exists. Hui Fei, who has read telegram with very happy expression, turns to Lily.

HUI FEI: *Are you going all the way to Shanghai?*
LILY: *Yes.*
HUI FEI: *So am I—and I am very happy about it*—
LILY: *So am I*—
HUI FEI (shy yet proud): *I'm going to be married when I arrive*—
LILY (with womanly interest and pleasure): *Are you very much in love with him?*
HUI FEI (simply): *yes, I am*—

DISSOLVE TO:

END OF SEQUENCE

ANATAHAN
(*THE SAGA OF ANATAHAN*)

Narration

The text which follows is that of the complete English commentary (written and spoken by Sternberg) that accompanies the images of the film and is superimposed on the sound track over the Japanese dialogue, thus obviating the need for subtitles. Besides translating the dialogue, usually in condensed form, although sometimes word for word when a particular point is accented, the commentary does just that, it comments on the action, not only in terms specific to the action but also in universal terms. "The Anatahan incident," said Sternberg, "gave me the opportunity to depict the Japanese not subjected to a Japanese problem which might not be understood abroad. The Japanese on Anatahan were part of a sudden misfortune which could happen to anyone anytime. And, therefore, this incident could help to bridge the distance between the legend of this country and the readiness (or lack of it) to understand this country by others." In short, not a Japanese film but an international film. Inspired by an actual episode of the late war in the Pacific, and adapted by the director from a book on the subject subsequently written by one of the survivors of "the battle of Anatahan," the commentary is written, as is the book, in the first person.

Nineteen days out of Yokohama, we were drifting toward Saipan at six knots an hour. The convoy consisted of five old bonito vessels. Our engines were in poor shape. We carried

badly needed supplies to our island outposts. We were fishermen, proud to be drafted into service, and had two soldiers
posted on each boat—no need for more we thought. We are
not prepared for defeat. Who is?

The lead boat, the Heiske Maru, was captained by an
old salt who knew nothing about this watery arena. His maps
showed some 2000 islands, like sprinkled crumbs on a vast
surface. We were now passing the Mariana archipelago. Once
it had belonged to Spain—then to Germany—and finally to
Japan, and we intended to keep it. This tropical world was
a geological joke of coral and volcano. Some islands lasted,
some disappeared. Some were inhabited, others were not.
Who would want to live here anyway? This giant body of
water, and all that was in it, was ours. Our belief in victory
was unshakable. We had stopped looking at the stepping
stones that paraded by—they were of no interest to us—we
wanted to return home.

We now sighted Anatahan—a jungle rock that stood high
out of the sleeping waters—so it was duly recorded in the
log that morning—June 12, 1944, the fourth year of a war
to which we had dedicated our lives, like children playing a
game without vision or foresight.

Four bells and our chief cook and bottle washer appeared
promptly with *asameshi*, breakfast for the skipper. His American sailor's hat was a reminder of a defeated enemy ship.

At first, we thought it was one of our own planes.

The barren map of the world makes no note of where misfortune strikes. We went down fast, few survived. The
Mariana trench over which we swam ashore was over 35,000
feet deep—the fiery center of the earth had blown this rock
of Anatahan a long way from the ocean floor. How we got
ashore, no one remembered. We were dumped like garbage
on a hot coast—left to rot—the change from a human being
with dignity to a helpless worm takes but a second. A merci-
ful narcosis kept us from suffering too much.

One of the men had not only saved his hide but accomplished the heroic feat of bringing a machine-gun ashore.
A warrant officer with a long service record—he was the only
one who knew what to do—to defend this island for a couple
of months was not a difficult task, he thought. He knew the
enemy, and he knew the Imperial Navy would not permit us
to stay abandoned very long.

Yes—we had picked the deepest part of the Pacific Ocean —deep and solemn.

We were to be here for seven long years and little did we know that the enemy was not in planes overhead, nor was it the lack of food, the lack of water and medicine—nor the venomous jungle that hemmed us in. How could we know that we had brought the enemy with us—in our own bodies —an enemy that would attack without notice.

One of our men had spotted a deserted village. This was good news, after many weeks of hardship.

And so we entered the twisting, haunted labyrinth of an unfamilar jungle—a beautiful but vicious world from which many of us never returned.

What kind of a Japanese was this? His name was Kusakabe —said he lived alone on the island—the others had left when the war started. He had been plantation foreman—exported copra—but the jungle had taken over—an unfriendly man, unfriendly to us—and unfriendly to himself.

Imagine living on an island like this by choice—thousands of miles from nowhere—all by himself—or was he all by himself?

That's how we met Keiko. At first, she was only another human being stranded on this pin-point on the map. Then, she was to become a female to us, and finally a woman—the only woman on earth.

REEL #2

The horizon stayed empty and remote. We lost track of time. The rains had started. They seemed never to end. We built boats—toy boats to carry us home on the wings of our longing. This lonely island was our whole world. We went to sleep at night and dreamt of home—each morning we were back on Anatahan.

Like a rare bird of the wet jungle—we caught an occasional glimpse of Keiko.

Some of us—sooner than the others, longed for something more than bread alone—and we watched her—and we watched each other.

The walls of the huts were thin. There were no secrets.

She had been out collecting shells as usual—his way of paying her a compliment was to call her "shell crazy."

The rains stopped—nothing lasts forever—though the waves of the ocean lasted long.

First thing we did when the hot rays of the sun came again was to build a Shinto Shrine to speed our prayers. Most of us believed in Shintoism. There were two Christians— four Buddhists—others believed only in Japan.

We extracted salt from the sea—hunted lizard and bat— found wild potatoes—lived on food that pigs would have rejected—but best of all, we found a way of making fire.

We had sunk to the level of prehistoric man—but our progress was not slow. We achieved in weeks what the cave man had taken centuries to accomplish.

And so we faced our new life—half way between Japan and New Guinea on a deserted sea-lane, 1500 miles from the Philippines—some 16 degrees above the Equator—resigned to wait.

The first typhoon struck us with an unjust fury. What had we done to reap all this? Why did man and nature conspire to make us helpless? The rocks that were so formidable when we crawled ashore were pebbles now in a giant sea. It raged for three days. The elements are cruel. To the winds and to the sea, man and his problems—is as nothing.

The typhoon pounded at us—the ocean wanted to wipe us out. The island rock that was anchored firmly to the bottom of the deep sea seemed to tear loose and join the storm.

One year on Anatahan! This was our home, now. Three miles long—one mile wide—most of it impenetrable. We stood guard in turns to wait for our Navy to come—it never came—for the enemy to come—he never came.

Nothing came but the waves—tides lifted and the tides fell. We watched the waves approach and we watched them recede, and we tried to find a meaning where there was none.

We now took another step away from prehistoric man. We had found empty beer bottles—and now we found a way of filling them—with coconut wine. If we drank quickly, before it turned to vinegar—it made us forget where we were and who we were.

We were scolded, of course, but since when has alcoholism been cured by scolding?

"Who are you combing your hair for?" "For you, naturally." Was she combing it for him?

Takahashi was the first man to break the social ice. He brought a peace offering. More shells for the wife as if she needed them. At that time, we still thought they were man and wife. And—we had not yet become savages.

The difference between a child and a grown-up is in the way the brain is in control of the emotions. Kusakabe objected to any one paying attention to Keiko. That was easy to diagnose—more difficult to understand was why he was so antagonistic—to us—and to himself.

Our leader, the boss of the island—that is, boss for a while, was not opposed to a display of his authority. Some men are drunk on wine—some are drunk on power.

So far, all these things that happened to us on Anatahan were small—our life now consisted of nothing but trifles. How were we to know what was important and what trifle was not?

She was a pretty woman—she was a Japanese woman—trained to obedience. When she was young, she followed her father—never dreamt of walking at his side. When she married, she walked behind the husband—obedience to a husband is considered to be the prime virtue of Japanese womanhood.

REEL #3

The full moon of the autumn equinox is the time for the "Ohigan" festival when we pay respect to our ancestors. Our thoughts then go from them to our families. The word Higan means the other shore. It is taken from the Buddhist legend that there is a river marking the division of this earthly world to a future one. This river is full of illusion, passion, pain, and sorrow. Only when you cross the river, having fought the currents of temptation to gain the far shore, do you reach enlightenment. This was the time when we thought of our families far away.

This was the time when we thought of our families—all of us—and so did Kusakabe. He had brought with him, when he came, wife and child. At the outbreak of the war, four years now—they had left him to go to Saipan—for safety. Keiko too had a husband who had left on the same boat. She too had not heard from him again. All this, we found out later.

Carelessly as we might wish to be in our human relations —there is a time of accounting.

Left alone in an empty world, it was natural for these two to have formed a bond of sorts—for a time they had forgotten everything but each other.

"Are you thinking of your home?" "Yes, but not when I see you." She was prepared to hear just that.

The longest journey begins with one step. Hers was to be quite a long journey.

This was Anatahan. We still kept track of the month, though we had forgotten the day of the week. A little while later, no one cared what year it was. Japan had forgotten us.

The horizon remained empty and remote, but the circle around Keiko enlarged; she was young, her body failed to remember the blows she had received. It also slipped her mind. She became better looking day by day. She became Queen Bee and the drones began to swarm.

"What's your husband doing?" "All I know, he's not out looking for another woman." "How would you like to be my bride tonight?" "I don't need two husbands."

Coconut wine had become our steady diet. With the coming of wine, discipline diminished. Some of us began to feel strongly about being told to stand guard day and night against an enemy that never came. Who was this man, anyway, who never allowed us to forget what it meant to be a Japanese soldier? All this talk of "stand up and salute" became more and more pointless.

It took him years to achieve his position, it took seconds to lose it.

Typhoons in human beings strike without much warning. There are few signals and only the skilled—the very skilled, can read them.

The loss of face to a soldier in command is not a pleasant experience. To lose the respect of our fellowmen is not pleasant to anyone—anywhere. A good part of our life is spent in trying to gain the esteem of others—to gain self-esteem, however, we usually waste little time.

REEL #4

We had thrown off the yoke of discipline. We were free—free of all restraint—which only meant that we were slaves to our bodies.

The *Tsundara Bushi*—an Okinawa folk song—had spread like a weed among the soldiers during the war.

"You and me—like an egg—I'm egg white, you're egg yellow, I embrace you."

The day started with a dispute over the words of a song. How the day would end, no one knew at the time. We were looking for trouble—and we found it.

"Keiko, Keiko . . . . come out, come out." Those were the right words!

Semba was 19, with the beard of a man and the brain of a grasshopper. He was next in line for Keiko's favors. We gave little thought to our actions. There is no medicine against stupidity—and it was epidemic among us.

Then came the unexpected!

"To all Japanese Forces! Three months ago—August 15—Japan accepted unconditional surrender. The Japanese Emperor himself is asking you to lay down your arms. The war is over. An American ship will take you home. Hostilities have ceased. All Japanese men and officers surrender—surrender at once!"

The unbelievable had happened. This could not be true. We had just begun the war. We were prepared to fight for a thousand years. We had overrun Asia, almost the entire Pacific—how could we have lost so suddenly?

This was an enemy trick. It could fool no one. We came to ask him to lead us again. There are those who lead and those who wish to be led. There is not necessarily any other bond between them.

"The sacred soil of Japan cannot be conquered. So long as we have one drop of blood in our veins—we will not give up. Rather die than surrender!"

But far away in Japan—our country had faced the reality of defeat. The Emperor had called the troops home. And millions streamed back—away from the nightmare of trying to conquer a world.

Father and son—wife and husband—mothers, daughters—
friends—all those who feared they might never meet again.
The men who had fought in vain came back home—there also
were many that did not come back.

REEL #5

But we knew nothing about what took place in a new
Japan. We were still on Anatahan—deserted by the world—
we were defending this volcanic rock—against what enemy?

The only real enemy most of us ever have is lonesomeness.

The jungle had disgorged a rare prize. An enemy plane had
been found wrecked, the bodies vanished.

This was a doubtful reminder of civilization. We fluttered
around this sudden gift from the skies like vultures—what
could we find to make our life better?

Some of the things were to make our life worse. Nishio
found a .45 calibre weapon and a few bullets—Yananuma,
too, hit the jackpot.

Keiko found a parachute—which meant elegance for us
instead of clothes made of tree-bark—or no clothes at all.

Semba, our friend, the lady-killer, found a ring—the easy
way to a woman's heart.

This lifeless mass of iron was the only sign of life from
the outside world, so far.

Maruyama was seaman first class. Before joining the Navy
he had been a first class musician. He had an idea how to
make use of rusty wire. He was to convert a war machine into
a musical instrument.

This was the first shot heard on the island—it was not to be
the last one—two old pistols—two new masters.

Keiko was gone. She had been missing all night. This was a
serious defection. Keiko missing? Kusakabe was more out of
his mind than usual.

Away from all our troubles—our now useless leader kept
the machine-gun ready to shoot. This gun was never to shoot.

Our search party went into action. Something must have
happened to Keiko—was she dead? We were too stunned to
count the men that were missing.

She was not dead—far from it—she was very much alive.
This was the beginning of a new pattern on Anatahan—Keiko

had gone into circulation. To spy on the humiliating details of another human being's life would be unforgivable were we not concerned in finding a clue to our own behavior. Nothing that happens to a human being is alien to us—there but for the grace of God go I.

Nishio and his friend are not uncommon among those that we know. They had guns now, to take the place of thinking.

Of course they had seen no one—why should they reveal her whereabouts—they had plans of their own. We had now been on this island for a long time, for all we knew we would be there forever. It is easy to look back and label all the commotion about Keiko ridiculous. What we did there— we might not have done somewhere else—opinions differ on that point—it is said that human beings react according to a set pattern whether they are in a primitive or a civilized society—maybe so. To look back on something is not the same as living with it.

The relationship between a man and a woman is based on emotions which often may not be understood by others—who in one way or another fumble just as much. It is easy to see what wrong others do—we carry no mirror to reflect our own actions.

REEL #6

She was clearly the winner this time—a bargain had been made. When a woman threatens to leave—this has considerable influence on the behavior of a man—even when she is not the only woman on earth.

Our leader took the occasion to lecture on our behavior— our mission was to defend Anatahan—not to drink and chase after females. Someday the enemy would appear. But he missed the most important point—the enemy *was* on Anatahan—man's genius to destroy himself was in clear evidence.

The day began with a harmless little ditty—a prelude to violence.

Keiko wanted to be taught how to play the shamisen. "What about your husband?" But she knew how to handle him now! One more blow out of him and she would leave him again!

We were all in bondage to Keiko—some more and some less. She was the center of our universe. We had no one to call our own—no one to care for us. It is not good for man to be alone.

Kuroda was the oldest sailor among us and he took the occasion to confirm our suspicions about the marital status of Keiko and Kusakabe—as if legalistic technicalities made any difference, any more, in Anatahan society. It was he who noticed the photograph—and told us about it later. There was no law on our island—no police—there were only two pistols.

Not so long ago these two had been members of the Imperial Navy—disciplined and polite—but the Navy was all but forgotten—and forgotten was what they had once been. But they were still human beings, and that classification is sufficient to cover quite a variety of behavior.

Certainly, Kusakabe had promised not to beat Keiko but in turn he reminded her that she had promised not to fool around with others. The two gunmen suggested that they settle their differences where they could be under scientific observation. They had an idea. Keiko could cook for four as easily as for two—Kusakabe could provide food if he wanted to be friendly. She did not object—too much. It would have done little good, if she had! Now these were no longer trifles. The knife and the bullet had become law.

So the Queen Bee kept house for three drones. At all these events that began now, we were not present. We were not inside that hut. There is no way to check the story of violence that now unfolded swiftly. Even had we been there—all our versions would differ.

One man who did try to check what occurred on the "hill of fools"—as we subsequently call this corner of the jungle— was our old friend Semba.

A little while later, his body was found in the swing where only a week before he had enjoyed the company of Keiko. We can only guess how he got into that hammock.

We can only surmise how a second body came to be found on that hill—two bullets buried deep in Nishio's back helped us to guess correctly.

In some parts of Asia there is a God of Immediate Retribution, whose function it is to spare us long delays in deserved

punishment. Had he decided to become the deity of Anatahan?

Anyway, death was fishing in this jungle and on his hook
as bait he dangled Keiko.

REEL #7

So we buried the two victims of our ill-fated mission with
due Shinto ceremony. A little part of us went down with them
into the moist ground. We felt sorry for the dead. Even an in-
sect an inch long has half an inch of soul. Time had stopped
for these two but our miserable existence continued.

We had now been on Anatahan for five years—five years
can be short—for us they were endless—days can be as fatal
as bullets—all that kept us alive was the thought of our
country.

Somewhere to the north was another island—an island that
we loved and longed for and could never forget as long as we
had breath in our bodies.

We celebrated the New Year like good Japanese soldiers.
We paid our respect in the direction of the Imperial Palace
and sang our National Anthem.

We wished each other a happy New Year—*omedeto
gozaimasu*—and as if nothing had happened, thanked each
other for the friendship of the past year and hoped courteously
that this year would be as pleasant as the last.

At all this, too, no one else was present. We can only reconstruct the events from which we were barred. The King
and Queen had left our festival—that we knew—but we never
saw the King again. He had been marked for death, indelibly,
long ago. The only thing we did not know was—who would
be the executioner?

Now Kusakabe was royalty. Anatahan had a new overlord—
a new King for a short time—for a short time only.

She followed him obediently—but this was a travesty of
obedience. Obedience at the point of a gun—is no obedience
at all.

We put Yananuma to rest. He died young. He had no
chance to learn how to live properly. Someday we would bring

his ashes back home—and lie to his people that he had died like a good soldier—honorably.

REEL #8

The Queen had returned to the beehive. But there was little rejoicing. They should have attended the funeral. You do not beat the dead.

When human beings wish to quarrel—they soon find a cause. The litany is of no consequence. This time it was: no food in the hut—why doesn't he go out and get some? There was no love in the hut also.

Next in line was the ex-cook of the Heiske Maru—Yoshiri. He aspired to Keiko—the goal of his ambitions was not lofty. We are driven by forces about which we know nothing.

The King is dead! What price the new King? How long will the tyrannical house of Yoshiri last? He was to wield his power over Anatahan for less than 24 hours. Keiko was his and all the coconut wine he could guzzle. Untold riches! But the Queen was not to be his. She had not been partial to the murder of her previous consort. The bond between them had been strong—whatever the nature of the elastic might have been that binds together male and female. He wanted her as Queen and handmaiden—no insolence—no one was going to throw a cup at his feet.

Would he have laughed quite so much had he known that he would not see the light of another day?

All of us remember that night. The moon was low—the trees silent. The air was full of mist—the sea was deep—the rocks black—Nature was indifferent to the cruel destiny of man.

The history of this unfortunate is the history of an American sailor's hat.

The two pistols were thrown into the ocean—they were gone. There was to be no more bloodshed—we chose Keiko peacefully, that is—peacefully, for us.

But Keiko was not going to be chosen peacefully or otherwise. She was through.

We started the hunt for the prize that this time had been won in fair competition.

The foe had found us—the long looked for enemy. We

were to be bombed—we thought—for this we had been trained—this was a simple matter.

"To the Japanese Army on Anatahan!" The "bombs" that had dropped told us that war had been over for five years—a vessel would call and take us home.

This was, of course, another crude enemy trick—what did they think we were—children?

REEL #9

This was hardly the time for love letters from the enemy—let's find Keiko!

We did not see this. We never saw her again. She disappeared as if she had never existed. Long ago, I heard her say that if she had wings she would fly home.

Keiko had gone—there was no more trouble—there was also no more life. And then a ship came and a white flag was found in our jungle burial ground. Letters from Japan.

This one was from Keiko. She had notified our families—told them we were alive—Kuroda had no family so she thoughtfully thanked him and said she hoped her departure had not brought too much trouble to him. This was embarrassing but definitely not an enemy trick.

There was another letter—from the Governor of the prefecture. "The war ended six years ago—your families are waiting—this flag we send has surrendered a Japanese regiment use it—we want you home!"

"You can return if you wish I will never go back to a defeated Japan!"

The rest of us surrendered—gladly. We had lost the battle of Anatahan.

We soared like eagles over our sacred mountain. It took 10 hours to retrace a journey of 19 days and seven long years.

We were back in Japan—heroes to all but to ourselves—brother and sister were there—our friends were waiting—father and mother—our neighbors came. We saw our wives—our children—now seven years older—we would have to earn their affection all over again—we were home at last.

And if I know anything at all about Keiko—she too must have been there.

Critical Reviews

Some Reflections on the Art of
Josef von Sternberg

So much has been written about Sternberg and his films that the director once remarked to me in real alarm that it was "inhuman." Perhaps in no countries more than America and France, however, have the most cogent and perceptive critical estimations and summings up of the Sternberg *daemon* been delineated. The following dozen excerpts (with the exception of a wry "pen portrait" published in London) appeared principally in New York and Paris. Trenchant and incisive, they have one thing in common: they attempt to get at the heart of the matter, e.g., his mordant art, so disconcertingly flecked with perverse humor as to, in the last analysis, confound even his most acute critics. A psychoanalyst, following the labyrinths of his psychological motivations, could conceivably throw up his hands in despair and say, "I can't figure out if he's in earnest or if he's kidding!"

Both, I'd say, but never at the same time—never.

Peter Balbusch
NOTES DURING THE FILMING OF
"SHANGHAI EXPRESS"
(extracts)

The night was glorious and one had to count it high in his favor. It is curious to think that all this exists only because a single brain wanted it to exist. The night, the searchlights,

Sternberg on the set for the opening scene of *Shanghai Express*
. . . . . "the intoxicating perfume of work" . . . . .

In nature, the crested crane; in the cinema, this, Dietrich garbed for her "Hot Voodoo" number in *The Blonde Venus*, a song, not a *danse lascif*, which another director would have made of such a costume. Ever present is the director's aesthetic equilibrium. (1932)

The art of the cigarette, a Dietrich specialty. Style is the servant of meaning, not an end in itself. In this portrait, Sternberg's meaning travels with the speed of light. Dietrich in *The Blonde Venus*—a tale, believe it or not, of mother love, like *The Case of Lena Smith*.

the dust, the wind—all this and the intoxicating perfume of
work, an actuality now—because *he* thought of it. At times
one can bodily feel how he thinks. I don't want to forget the
locomotive that blew its puff of white steam into a yellow
sky. It was unspeakably beautiful in this barren landscape.

. . .

They slander him a good deal and one is either for or
against him. Curiously enough, there is not even the typical
American well-tempered tolerance for success. So definite is
his personality, one must either love or hate him and when
you love him you smilingly accept all that which arouses
antagonism in others.

. . .

Polished dialogue? The hell with it! To the capable director dialogue is no more than a spoken musical note of the
final theme, infinitely varied and harboring hundreds of unspoken meanings.

. . .

Even the camera and the microphone can be inspired
through barely noticeable movement and their own obstinate
qualities, and I believe that the future directors will take
strong advantage of the ideas proposed by the stubborn film
machinery.

. . .

It would be interesting to find out what some of the
Chinese extras think about the filming, the director, and the
complicated apparatus. Probably we would all come off badly.

. . .

What I admire in him is not his cinematic genius that reveals itself in his bird-of-prey eyes and his lightning com-
prehension and control of any situation. That can be learned
and may often be harbored in an individual. But what counts
most and makes him great is his endurance, his mind forcing
domination over his threadbare nerves, his stoicism and monk-
like humility toward his work.

*Written on a copy of the shooting
script on the sets during the
filming of "Shanghai Express."
Hollywood, Autumn, 1931*

Charles Graves

JOSEF VON STERNBERG

Josef von Sternberg walks like a cat, looks like a fallen archangel, wears Mongolian moustachios and black Chinese pyjamas, is never seen out of doors without a walking-stick, craves cornflowers, and always expects the head waiters to bring, unasked, seven iced black grapes when he enters a restaurant. He has wavy grey hair, steel-blue eyes, a horror of the cold, and a consequent love of the tropics. He talks epigrammatically, paints admirably, and has already sculptured his own tombstone—a brooding, monkish figure holding its head with one hand. The only things he has not yet done are to write his own epitaph or to direct Charles Laughton. And he is beginning on the latter early in the New Year.

Mr. von Sternberg lives at the Splendide, resents being put under the slightest obligation by strangers, always refers to Marlene Dietrich as "Miss Dietrich," visits lunatic asylums wherever he can find them, and has built himself an all-steel house in the San Fernando Valley. Here he has a valuable collection of portraits by Utrillo, as well as by Van Gogh, Picasso, Modigliani, and most of the other leading modern painters.

Born in Vienna of Polish and Hungarian parents forty-two years ago, he emigrated to the United States at the age of seven. Always possessed with a leaning toward chemistry, he found himself in the film industry on the laboratory side. Soon he became a film patcher, and finally was put in charge of the camera department. Today, he is the only director who has a union card as a camera-man. Not only that, he cuts and edits his own films. It was he who discovered Miss Dietrich, took her to America, directed her first six pictures, and earned the title of "Marlene's Svengali." He also gave their first real chance to Evelyn Brent, Herbert Marshall, Warner Oland, Gary Cooper, William Powell, George Bancroft, Victor McLaglen, Sylvia Sidney, Cary Grant, and Cesar Romero. *I, Claudius* will not be the first English picture with which he will have been associated. Fourteen years ago he was an

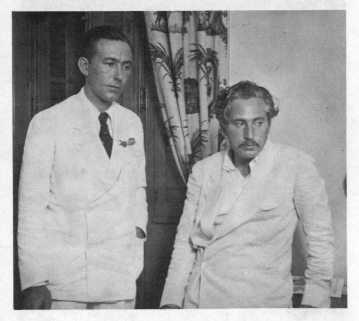

Paul Ivano, cameraman for *The Sea Gull*, and Von Sternberg, just before taking off for the Caribbean to shoot a hurricane for the next Dietrich film, but the hurricane failed to materialize and the project was abandoned. (1932)

Yes, the future has definitely arrived. Director and star, the subjects of more éclat than any team in screen history, dine out in Holly-wood. They are at the pinnacle of their success. (1934)

assistant director at Twickenham, with the Alliance Film Company. Previously, during the war, he had been appointed motion-picture expert to the American G.H.Q. and taught them bayonet fighting on the screen. The picture that made him famous was *The Salvation Hunters*—and was incidentally the only one of his own he ever saw with an audience—which laughed.

Josef von Sternberg is ultra-sensitive to noise (he once told Miss Dietrich to stop her teeth chattering), secretive, cynical, and certain of himself. He says truthfully that he is neither morbid, sinister, nor particularly decadent. He is merely a realist. He thinks deeply, never evades issues, and enjoys trying to disconcert you. Quite incidentally, he is the greatest living director.

The Bystander, London
Dec. 9, 1936

Kirk Bond

JOSEF VON STERNBERG REVISITED

. . . I think that, if anything, his stature increases. He is, beyond question, one of the great directors. He ranks in this country with Vidor, with Lubitsch, perhaps only a little below Griffith and Stroheim. . . . He is one of the richest, one of the subtlest of directors. He may not always be easy to follow, but to those who are ready to follow he is immensely rewarding. He combines, in a way that may be unique in art, a luxurious pictorial style with a detached, often sardonic point of view that seems almost grotesquely at odds with the warm imagery. But that is Sternberg . . .

Sternberg is a poet who writes of life as he sees it, standing somewhere off at the side, understanding, criticizing, yet loving it, too. And it is part of Sternberg that his love comes out in little tender moments almost awkwardly—and yet is so vital and basic to the whole fabric.

"You see," says Menjou in *Morocco*, "they love their men." "Perhaps," says Marlene in *Dishonored*, "[I did it] because I love him." Such tiny, almost Chinese-like cameos are worth more than vast epics of tumultous red passion.

A similar moment occurs in the opening scene of *Dis-*

honored. Marlene stands on the sidewalk as what appears to be a suicide is carried out. Someone in the small crowd growls, "They all end that way." In a tone that is indescribable Marlene says, "No, they don't!" Of course they don't. It is part of the dogma of our hard age that they *do*, and one of the wonderful things about Sternberg is that he has the courage and the compassion to say they don't.

And then there comes the other Sternberg, worldly, sardonic, but never cynical. "What a lovely evening we might have had," says Warner Oland in *Dishonored* with the meditative calm of a Buddhist monk, "if you weren't a spy and I a traitor." "Then," replies Dietrich, "we might never have met."

In the midst of the swooningly beautiful hubbub of the duel in *The Devil Is a Woman*, Edward Everett Horton as the mayor (complete with trim beard) arrives. "Good morning, gentlemen." (It is raining pitchforks.) "A pretty mess." And a few minutes later: "All professions have their compensations, even mine." Shaw could hardly do better.

The wonderful endings of *Morocco* and *Dishonored* deserve a special note. They are not to be excused or brushed aside as too bizarre. They are essential parts of Sternberg's work. And they bring tears to the eyes . . .

Film Courier, New York
Summer, 1959

Andrew Sarris

THE CINEMA OF JOSEF VON STERNBERG

The cinema of Von Sternberg is the cinema of illusion and delusion, of men deluded by women, of men and women deluded by surface appearances. Von Sternberg has always worked within a studio enclosure where he could control the lighting and texture. When a French interviewer asked him why he had constructed a studio set for the Pacific Island of *Anatahan*, Von Sternberg replied simply, "Because I am a poet." Some critics have mistakenly confused his poetry with folly as if Von Sternberg himself had been as deluded as his characters . . . Von Sternberg the man undoubtedly shared some of the follies of his characters, but Von Sternberg the director never lost his formal grip on his material. The critical sentiment in the Thirties was that films were supposed to be short, snappy, and to the proletarian point. Von Sternberg was thus considered slow, decadent, and self-indulgent, and gloriously ambiguous Marlene Dietrich was judged too rich for the people's blood. This was a time for bread, not cake. Today, Von Sternberg and Dietrich look more dazzling than ever while most of the cinema of the bread lines looks excessively mannered. Time invariably vindicates form over topicality, and poetry always outlives journalism.

Film Culture, New York, Spring, 1963

Jack Smith

A BELATED APPRECIATION OF J.V.S.

People never know why they do what they do. But they have to have explanations for themselves and others.

So Von Sternberg's movies had to have plots even though they already had them inherent in the images. What he did was make movies naturally—he lived in a visual world. The explanations, plots he made up out of some logic having nothing to do with the visuals of his films. . . .

In this country the movie is known by its story. A movie is a story, is as good as its story. Good story—good movie. Unusual story—unusual movie, etc. Nobody questions this. It is accepted on all levels, even "the film is a visual medium" plane, by its being held that the visuals are written first then breathed to life by a great cameraman, director. In this country the blind go to the movies. There is almost no film an experienced and perceptive blind man couldn't enjoy. This is true. I was a Broadway barker once and was approached by a blind man! The B.M. was right—there must be others! The manager, nobody, thought it strange—at the time I didn't— and don't now. I do think it strange that nobody uses their eyes. . . .

I don't think Von Sternberg knew that words were in his way, but he felt it—and he invested his images with all the care he rightfully denied the words. And he achieved the rich-

est, most alive, most right images of the world's cinema—
in company with men like Von Stroheim, the genius of *Zero
de Conduite*, early Lang, and that limited company....

Possibly he might have been afraid of reaction if it were
known that his visual fantasy world was really his own mind.
He might have deliberately obscured, distracted attention
from the shock that might have occurred, if his creation had
been understood through the eye. To close the ears would
have thrown the viewer into an undersea, under-conscious,
world where the realities were very different from what the
script purported. He needn't have worried. As it was, no one
had that ability to see. He was misunderstood and well understood. Well understood in that his covert world disturbed;
misunderstood in that no one knew why or appreciated the
wonder of being disturbed. Misunderstood and done an in-
justice to in that finally, when opinion turned against him,
it was for the wrong reason: (wrong not because people
should not be disturbed) the "insipid stories, bad acting, bad
dialogue," etc. Wrong reasons because they were, to be true
to his expression, deliberately "bad." Then he was punished
—turned out of Hollywood and never again allowed to work.
Only frightened people punish. Ostensibly because he had
violated good technique. Good technique being used as something people hide behind when they are frightened by
something they wouldn't like in themselves, therefore *is* in
themselves. And the hypocrisy of good acting, good this,
good that—GOOD MOVIES being perpetuated—GOOD
EMPTY—BANAL—UNTRUE MOVIES—IMPERSONAL
MOVIES.

Film Culture, New York
Winter, 1963–64

Ado Kyrou

STERNBERG AND THE MARLENE MYTH

There never was a more exalting association than that between Sternberg and Marlene. But to be more accurate, let
us say right away that Marlene only exists through Sternberg,
just as the work of this genial director only exists through
her and for her.

The next was a mad stunt, a "Carnaval Russe" on the theme of
Catherine II ("the Great") with the Imperial Court peopled by
gargoyles both human and sculptured, a film-*toccata* of relentless
brio crackling with insolent wit. Sam Jaffe as the Grand Duke Peter
and Dietrich as the newly arrived Sophia Frederika. *The Scarlet
Empress.* (1934)

Byzantine luxury. Louise Dresser as the Empress Elizabeth admonishes her half-wit son, Peter (Sam Jaffe), as his bride-to-be, Sophia Frederika (Dietrich), looks on. *The Scarlet Empress.*

Detail from the wedding of Peter and Sophia Frederika in the Cathedral of Kazan, according to the Russian Orthodox ceremony. Done entirely *sans* the vocal ritual but accompanied by Rubenstein's "Kamenei Ostrow" as a musical interpretation of the ritual. *The Scarlet Empress.*

"Exit Peter—enter Catherine!" The procession following Peter's assassination, which heralds the ascendancy of Catherine to the throne. Dietrich in hussar's uniform as a symbol of the male power she will assume. *The Scarlet Empress*.

He used to say: "Cinema is a commercial profession which utilizes tools that could have been used for the creation of art." He and the few true men of the cinema (Chaplin, Eisenstein, Vigo, Buñuel, Fields) dared and were lucky enough to be able to utilize these tools to express themselves freely. They understood that only their personal vision of the world was of capital interest. Incapable of abiding by the commercial exigencies (he had innumerable problems with producers and critics), Sternberg gave us his world without worrying about the ridiculous question of true and false, real and unreal. His world, like any personal world charged with magnetism, is a mirror that we cannot grasp with our feeble means; the communion can only come about with sensivity. Sternberg's truth is beyond the subject matter, the people, and the ideas, and even when he makes a film imposed on him, he cannot help filming it in his own universe of dreams. Sternberg's universe, made up of the unusual and of eroticism, is purely surrealistic: he burns its visible envelopes with corrosive rays in order to explore its latent riches.

His first picture, *The Salvation Hunters*, was realized and produced with amateur means, but it already reveals that which will make Sternberg's majesty. The poetic aspect of things dominates the manifest aspect and man's forces (nonphysical) are its subject matter. Each gesture, each spoken sentence is transfigured, a predominant search already appears, the search for the woman which will enable Sternberg to leave the *"marie-salope"* of *Salvation Hunters* and nearly find the ideal in *Underworld*. In it Evelyn Brent has the symbolic name of *"Feathers,"* light and present, like the feathers she leaves in her path; she will make the killer, Bancroft, understand in one hour what a whole lifetime could not have taught him. A year later, Bancroft, a rough sailor in *The Docks of New York*, will meet a woman, Betty Compson, whom he will not immediately recognize as The Woman. He believes she is but a companion for the night and in the morning, while she is still asleep, he gets up to go after leaving her a few dollars on the night-table, but he turns around, looks at Betty's beautiful body, smiles, and adds two dollars. He comes back later and the couple unites in a real, mad love, braving the ribbing and the obstacles that surround them. "The rules of the established morality are not respected for a moment—the heart, pleasure, pride, a sense of personal dignity are the only rulers of the people in this story." (J. G. Auriol, *Revue du Cinéma*, 1929). Now Sternberg knows the object of his desperate search; in the extraordinary *Case of Lena Smith* he enumerates the obstacles and the ignominious ways in which love is forbidden.

He goes to Germany in 1930 to make a picture based on a novel by H. Mann. It is the story of a beautiful woman and of a man who will live only for her, despite the consequences of this love. Sternberg thinks of Gloria Swanson or of Phyllis Haver for the main role, but in the musical show, *Zwei Krawatten (Two Neckties)*, he notices a young singer who had already tried her luck in pictures, but failed to make it despite her interpretation in an unjustly forgotten film, *The Isle of Lost Ships* by Tourneur. Her name is Marlene Dietrich. She is The Woman and Sternberg makes her get up on the studio sound stage so that her legs can better be seen, he surrounds her with female "horses" to show off her beauty, he caresses her with his camera, with his lights, with his shadows, as no woman has ever been caressed before.

From now on Sternberg's work will be Marlene. He creates her in the image he has of her, he places her in his universe, he explodes with joy, his cries of happiness come up magnificent. He shows us his exultant happiness: it is not just a woman, it is not life as you believe you live it, it is Sternberg's woman in Sternberg's life, which changes everything. His reticence is over, Sternberg no longer searches, he has found, he will now make passionate films.

This huge gorilla who staggers onto a cabaret stage will pull off his ridiculous attire and Marlene, superb, will appear (*Blonde Venus*). A mad king drills holes in the eyes of sculpted angels on the walls to watch Marlene, who gets undressed next door (*The Scarlet Empress*). The burning desert sand becomes a moving rug under Marlene's feet (*Morocco*). Marlene is offered the most beautiful accessories, the maddest poses, she walks around the grottoes in a white lace dress (*Blonde Venus*). A clothes madness comes over Sternberg: a lunacy unequaled in the history of cinema, he braves all criticism concerning his "bad taste," he dresses Marlene in the most unusual and most erotic manner. I was never able to enumerate Marlene's outfits in *Shanghai Express*.

With such a woman events cannot follow their usual course; the unusual, the surrealistic, accompany her, and huge

How can you follow a bravura work like *The Scarlet Empress* without its being an anti-climax? For this was to be their last film together. You make the exasperatingly sado-masochistic *The Devil Is a Woman* because as you get older, she get's more and more beautiful. Something (someone?) has to give. Dietrich and goose, Lionel Atwill. (1935)

"Marlene is not Marlene, she is me," Sternberg once said. So was everyone else who ever acted in his films. Their composite is a portrait of the director more accurate than any single camera portrait of him can show. Dietrich as the devastating Concha Perez of *The Devil Is a Woman*, played in high parody and a stylized *tour de force*.

That ball of fire, the sun, gives light, and men have learned to manipulate light incandescently. Put to the service of the pan-sexual morality of Sternberg, in terms of the most silken chiaroscuro, the effect is truly promethean. Louys, from whose *Woman and Puppet* the story derives, left one man gutted at the end. Sternberg leaves two. Dietrich and Cesar Romero (as Don Antonio). *The Devil Is a Woman*.

White on white—sheer opalescence. Here the camera literally paints with light and the lattice-work on the door seems as if done with a painter's brush. Vermeer eliminated the brush-stroke in painting; Sternberg puts the brush-stroke in photography. Opposites become one. Dietrich in *The Devil Is a Woman*.

marble gargoyles lead her steps. If she is a spy, she will commit treason against her country to be faithful to her love (*Dishonored*) and in a make-believe Spain she becomes the frenzied heroine of a wildly romantic story (*The Devil Is a Woman*).

Sternberg now reigns over his own films, nothing will oust him. Thanks to *the* woman, he has achieved a sublime freedom and with ferocious joy he makes pictures, just as great poets write poetry for themselves. "My pictures are acts of arrogance," he used to say.

Then came Sternberg's separation from the ideal woman he had created. His universe should normally have become empty; the creator was so involved with the laces and jewels that covered his creature, the love between creator and creature was so strong, that they fused into one being (I mean in their pictures, I do not mention what may have happened outside their films). Sternberg feels lost for six years, his pictures still have the magnetic imprint of his universe, but he is obviously filming "to do his job." Yet it seems that his picture, *I, Claudius*, might have been a masterpiece.

Suddenly, in 1941, he makes *Shanghai Gesture* without Marlene and again this is very great Sternberg. He makes his picture, perhaps his most personal one, with melo-theatrical means. Through a curious sexual and cinemato-graphic mechanism he makes it a Marlene picture, her presence is felt (I nearly said that one smells her perfume), she is "seen" but she is now a split person: she is Gene Tierney, all woman with her unkempt hair; she also is Victor Mature, the man Sternberg himself. This Doctor Omar, "doctor of nothing, poet of Shanghai—and Gomorrah," has Marlene's lascivious poses, her great cruelty, her voluptuousness, but he is also Sternberg, himself, who made Marlene and who will be instrumental in the plot destined to crush Marlene—Gene Tierney.

A clever and instinctive complexity has always recreated the same woman in Sternberg's personal world. She appears again as Jane Russell in *Macao*. Sternberg had created a myth; he can no longer escape it. Sternberg and Marlene were never really separated. And if they now made a film together?

Josef von Sternberg is the most complex of *cinéastes*. He is also the most misunderstood. His flamboyant originality

Sternberg follows his former producer at Paramount, B.P. Schulberg, to Columbia Pictures, for whom he makes a perfunctory *Crime and Punishment*, after Dostoievski, and since it is not his adaptation and he lacks his usual autonomy, the picture looks it. Peter Lorre (Raskolnikov) and Marian Marsh (Sonia). (1935)

His follow-up picture for Columbia is *The King Steps Out*, from the Fritz Kreisler operetta, *Cissy*. Grace Moore (Cissy, afterwards Empress Elizabeth of Austria) and Franchot Tone (Franz Josef, afterward Emperor) on a spree in the Prater. (1936)

Sternberg returns from a trip around the world to direct *I, Claudius* for Alexander Korda in London. In high leather safari boots and Hindu turban he is, at first, an intimidating sight on the set. Later, his graciousness will dispel all his cast's fears. (1937)

Charles Laughton (as the imbecilic Roman emperor, Tiberius Claudius Drusus) and Flora Robson (as his mother, the Empress Dowager, Livia). Laughton, though marvelous in the part, develops some eccentricities that contribute toward the abandonment of the film in its early stages. (1937)

Emlyn Williams as Caligula in *I, Claudius*—seldom has evil incarnate been so acidly portrayed. The eyes of a basilisk in a human face. Sternberg later said it might have been his best work had he been given the chance to finish it.

After a number of non-realized projects, Sternberg returns to Hollywood to fulfill an old contract with MGM where he is assigned a
picture to which he is totally unsympathetic. "There is nothing of
me in it," he said. Wallace Beery in *Sergeant Madden*. (1939)

But he is back in Hollywood again, and in this photo with old friends at Ciro's. L. to R.—René Clair (then directing Dietrich in *The Flame of New Orleans*), the lady herself, Joe Pasternak, that film's producer, and Sternberg. (1941)

Then "from out of the blue" comes the offer to direct with complete autonomy again, as in the old days. An all but impossible assignment—the lurid *The Shanghai Gesture*—whose deadly attack on moral hypocrisy had somehow to be deflected to pass the censors. Sternberg's adaptation fooled them—and no one else. Notable for the hieratic beauty of Gene Tierney (Poppy) and the corrosive spleen of Ona Munson, Sternberg's "Chinese Dietrich," as "Mother Gin-Sling." (1941)

Next came an assignment about an American jet ace and a female Soviet jet ace for Howard Hughes, *Jet Pilot*, Sternberg's first color film, and a comedy (his only one). Some amusing "aerotics" were almost the only sternbergian touches that survived the wholesale reshooting and re-editing this picture suffered. John Wayne and Janet Leigh were starred. (1951, but not released till 1957)

A second assignment for Mr. Hughes was *Macao*, about diamond smugglers in the mysterious East. Despite Sternberg's previous successes with exotic locales, the picture was almost totally reshot by another director (Nicholas Ray). Only some telling atmospheric shots remained of Sternberg's work. Jane Russell starred (with Robert Mitchum). William Bendix is her vis-à-vis here. (1951)

places him outside commercial limitations. The unusual, the
magic, the eroticism of his films, lead us beyond everything.
The elements of his subject matter only lead us, however
rationally, toward the irrational. He minutely details events
that are of minor importance in order to get to scenes that
take place in the depths of the unexplored. I think of the
final sequence in *Morocco*, of the demonic faces in *The Case
of Lena Smith*, of the dinner in *Shanghai Gesture*, where a
lame man plays a romantic tune on the piano while a giant
coolie opens the window, enabling the customers to see half-
naked women hanging high up in birds' cages; the chase
through the labyrinth of the fisherman's nets in *Macao*, and
of all the other images that constitute this unique entity in
the history of cinema. His lashes wake our numbness, his
flashes of light touch the innermost depths of our sensitivity,
while his work remains that immense and marvelous hymn to
woman and to love.

"Here nothing is impossible!" says one of his protagonists.
Eroticism upsets daily habits and a perpetual carnival is
bound to release its monsters.

Sternberg's last picture, *The Saga of Anatahan*, is, perhaps,
more disconcerting than even his preceding masterpieces.
Total author (he directed it, wrote the scenario, narrated it,
and photographed it), the great director went to Japan to
film the true story of twelve Japanese sailors who, isolated on
a jungle island, continue to believe for years that the war is
not yet over. But he realized that the settings of Japan were
not what he wanted so he built a jungle in a studio and he
himself painted "Japanese clouds" for his sets. This is one
of those rare films in the history of cinema in which sexual
desire is the only subject matter, because, before these men,
isolated from the rest of the world, is a young and beautiful
woman whom Sternberg calls "The Queen Bee." The sailors
all sing around her: "You and I, like an egg—you, egg yellow:
I, egg white—I embrace you!" Sea shells, jungle vegetation,
and exacerbated feelings take us back into Sternberg's world,
while we cannot help noticing an unusual calm, a calm dis-
tilled of passion, which reminds us of the same kind of calm
in Buñuel.

Le surréalisme au cinéma, Éditions
Arcanes, 1953, re-published by
Éditions du Terrain Vague, 1963.

René Jeanne and Charles Ford

PRIMITIVE VIOLENCE

The three pictures, *Underworld, Docks of New York, Dragnet*, form a homogeneous ensemble, which one seldom finds in the work of an American director, and in that respect Sternberg is set apart from Stroheim, who despite his intransigency—and perhaps because he had a richer personality—tried his luck in very different directions. With *Underworld* Sternberg found the climate that suited him. Very reasonably, he stuck to it and he is perhaps best judged on these three pictures because he feels at ease only when he is confronted with violently dramatic action. He does not care whether or not his characters resemble those of headline stories, as long as the filmic life he has to struggle with is ardent, and he is quite indifferent if it happens to be brutal and sordid. The personages he most incisively animates are those who are devoid of complications and psychological subtleties, and who are moved by primitive feelings of extreme violence—as one finds them in the romantic repertory. Georges Charensol does not hesitate to say of them that "like the heroes of antiquity, fate destines them to the worst catastrophies." However, these characters are never simple, because their animator knows how to enrich them throughout the action that motivates them, without being obvious about it and without ever slowing down that action. From the very start he holds his public in thrall and doesn't let go until he has achieved a knockout. The screen had never presented anything similar to its faithful under anybody's signature, unless it was under Stroheim's. One must add for another thing that Sternberg never lost the qualities for which Paramount first hired him, as "technical adviser for lighting and photography," e.g., he was a virtuoso of lighting, particularly when he had to compose in chiaroscuro. On the other hand, he knew at least as well as Griffith how to get the best out of his actors—it is not an exaggeration to say that he revealed Bancroft to himself, that he discovered Evelyn Brent, and that under his direction Olga Baclanova was once a very fine screen actress. These are some of the reasons—the least debatable—which make Sternberg one of the great men of the American cinema during that richly creative period that preceded the advent of the sound film.

Histoire Encyclopédique du cinéma,
Vol. 3, *Le Cinéma Americaine,*
Éditions Robert Laffont, 1965.

Philippe Demonsablon

A HEART LAID BARE

If one looks at *The Saga of Anatahan* it presents the example of a fight between hazardous production circumstances and a definite will to create, between a poverty of means to realize and the density through which the author expects to express himself. But the picture also presents a definite triumph of one over the other—a just revenge if one remembers to what extent Sternberg's career had been upset almost twenty years before and if one imagines the feeling of a creator to whom creating has been denied. However these years of silence and of half-silence were not in vain and now Sternberg gives us with *Anatahan* a mature work, with a more demanding precision and a more complex design than ever. For this work has two closely connected aspects, each one of which corresponds to the feelings it inspires: first in the succession in which we see the images, with their own powers of fascination, which justifies the admiration one has for them; then the reflection, or rather the projection, extremely willful, of the man who created them. These two levels will facilitate the understanding of what has been achieved.

The newspapers have published this ridiculous and tragic episode of the last war: a group of fishermen and Japanese soldiers were stranded on the island of Anatahan in 1944. With the exception of one couple, the island was deserted. Refusing to believe that Japan had been defeated, they waited for the arrival of the enemy who no longer existed, they ended up by fighting among themselves for the possession, they thought, of the woman. This went on for seven years. It could just as well still be going on while I write these lines. Based on these true events of our time, and with great respect for the truth, Sternberg conceived a work decidedly nonrealistic. The film offers many examples of this: the most striking ones showing that provocation is always present, also a certain aristocratic pleasure to displease; but it displeases only the stupid ones. And as if to baffle completely those who might misunderstand, Sternberg went across the Pacific to build a jungle set in a Kyoto studio, probably a small one, because he is more at ease when confined to little space (one remembers *Shanghai Gesture* and the docks setting of *Macao*), and he engaged a troupe of Kabuki dancers to play the actors of this drama.

One already conceives what transfiguration this procedure accomplished. The author thus acquired a greater freedom to express a poetic truth. What could be more abstract than this arid and parched jungle, rather than the steaming jungle we have seen in so many films? There were still other conventional things that had to be done away with. First of all, the dramatic conventions—and the style of the actors' playing contributes to eliminate those. A unique thing in a "Japanese film": expressive gestures have been replaced by the magic of their looks, often directed at the prodigious unknown of their vision. One cannot help recognizing the stylization of the German movie men, Fritz Lang and Murnau, who are much more concerned with plunging their characters into an abstract universe than confronting them with each other. This effacement of all dramaturgic structure is accentuated by the commentary throughout the duration of the film. I presume that this procedure was deemed necessary for the exploitation of the film in the United States. But Sternberg himself wrote this commentary and it is his voice we hear for one and a half hours over the images; this was not just to sum up the speech of the characters, but to comment upon their actions, thus introducing a time-lag between the images and the thoughts regarding the images. These actions are even announced in advance quite often and the dramatic interest then gives place to a stupefied feeling of fatality; the account becomes a horrible and necessary ceremony that gives reality to the words of the one who gives the account. In short, if the commentary could invite the attitude of a moralist, such an attitude is quickly bypassed. It is impossible here to attain, or to keep, the detachment which moralists try to have

and which often is only coldness; the images of passion on
the screen would immediately contradict it, and the spectator thus solicited in contrary directions by the images and
the commentary (or should we say by the commentary and
its images) cannot help having a bad conscience in this
duality.

But we must not go any further if we want to explain a
feeling that owes everything to a work of such sincerity, a
work that Sternberg created with such meticulous care. It even
seems as if he had made *The Saga of Anatahan* primarily for
himself. The spectator is an intruder in the theatre, but since
he is now involved, let him into the secret, even if it is one
he did not want to hear.

I know that those who consider even an artistic production
solely as a means of entertainment will be indignant that behind the work one is curious about the man who created it
and that through this work one attempts to communicate
with him. But isn't man a phenomenon surprising enough
so that all the aspects of his activity are worthy of our interest? What do I get out of listening to all those brilliant con-
versationalists who can tell me nothing? I prefer the company of Rossellini, Aldrich, Sternberg, and a few others.
Those are my dear friends; even the shadows of their anxious
faces speak to me from the screen. *The Saga of Anatahan*
appears to me like that impossible work Edgar Allan Poe
wanted to write and call "My Heart Laid Bare"; indeed, the
screen is nearly in shreds and ablaze from the fulminations
that Sternberg projects on it and that, without a doubt, come
from deep within him. Although it offers us some thoughts
on the meaning of existence, this reverie is not satisfied to
give us merely the fruit of an experience. The dream itself
becomes a subject for our reflection. In his soliloquy, the narrator retraces his experience, he observes it with detachment,
as if brooding over what was unique and irreversible in it. An
erotic experience of which Woman is the center, inevitable
source of fascination, object of adoration and terror that inspires cruel and impossible divinities, her erotic power crowns
her Queen, or Goddess; her dwelling is a temple decorated
with the multitudinous fetishes of the Woman, and these
adorn every gesture of hers, a ritual her court observes with
fervor.

Absolute and inaccessible sovereign, her power destroys

those who come near her; but she is also only a ridiculous means because she did not seek this power and the men who surround her are determined to see her dethronement and her destruction through the myth they created to maintain their passion. Thus Keiko joins Sternberg's most famous heroines. It is known how the seven years of his "baudelairian" concept of Woman made him idolize Marlene Dietrich and how several years later he chose an actress in the image of the other: Ona Munson. Twenty years later, in *The Saga of Anatahan*, we "meet" Sternberg himself in the person of the husband. The knot to *The Blue Angel* is here tied, and it is probably not by chance that the account of the same humiliations appear in the same scenes. But this time Sternberg *lived* them and he put into them an all but unbearable veracity. Without a doubt, the husband's frightened look, his fits of panic and submissiveness, would be impossible to watch if such scenes did not enable Sternberg to look back lucidly and without illusion at the sorceries of his own past.

"The relationship between husband and wife is based on sentiments, often misunderstood by others, whose behavior, however, is not less blameable," a 60-year-old Sternberg tells us, while a 35-year-old Sternberg on the screen falls to his knees before his wife, who walks away. Let's remember the lesson. The essential thing is to grow old gracefully, but it also is more difficult.

Cahiers du Cinéma, No. 58, April, 1956

Henri Agel

It would be just as inopportune to gauge Sternberg according to his coefficient of social reality and his "negating anarchy" as it would be incongruous to evaluate *Les Fleurs du Mal* from the point of view of nineteenth-century historic truth. We do not cite Baudelaire by chance. There is more than one affinity between the author of "Spleen de Paris" and the director of *The Shanghai Gesture*: cruel masochism that explodes in *The Devil Is a Woman* (whose protagonist, Lionel Atwill, physically resembles Sternberg, vampirized by Marlene Dietrich), an ambivalence sustained by a morbid voluptuousness with regard to the woman, perverse and insensitive goddess, who reigns in insolent splendor, enhanced by make-up, jewels, and the most vertiginous costumes: this taste for carnival and disguise used to obsess Baudelaire and the theme of the androgyne appeared in *Les Journaux Intimes* as it does in *The Blonde Venus*.

Just as the poet Sternberg seems to abhor everything "natural." Therefore his metamorphosis of the 1929 Marlene, plump and slightly bovine. It did not suffice him to hollow her cheeks, to widen the look of her eyes like those of an opium smoker, he invented for her mythological moltings of garb, each more fabulous than the other, the total effect of which was delirious with exhibitionism. *The Blonde Venus* would have been the apotheosis of the erotic, with all the phases of decadence illustrated by glittering rags among which there is the barbaric outfit of a gorilla, had there not been *The Scarlet Empress*, a kind of petrified parade of Russian-American music hall, in which the sexual awakening and awareness of her power makes Catherine's itinerary the reverse of that of Lola Montez. But the swan song of this duo, which defied the most extravagant wagers, was a dreamlike and funereal adaptation of Pierre Louys's novel, *Woman and Puppet*. The Vamp, incarnated here by Concha Perez, a species of super-Carmen, hideous as a result of so much cruel and metallic splendor, evoked those devouring females of the Italian silent screen as in d'Annunzio's deliriums. She appears at the end all in black, adorned with sinister magnificence, shortly before which she has sung a ballad the very German sadism of which blends well with the atmosphere of a decadent Spain, just as Cocteau might have dreamed it. An image where one could easily recognize the fusion of Goya and Léonor Fini, the implacable triumph of a funereal Eros, as imagined by Pierre Jean-Jouve, and the crystallization of the haggard and tormented imagination of an obsessed dream.

Ado Kyrou, who consecrated a very beautiful chapter to Sternberg in his book, *Amour, Erotisme et Cinéma*, sees in this film the hopeless expression of erotic potency in woman.

Between the suicidal lyricism of *The Devil Is a Woman* and the infernal engulfment of *Shanghai Gesture* there is no discontinuity. There is, however, one difference. The "femme fatale" who clothed her bewitching carnality in all climates, the aridity of Africa (*Morocco*), the Vienna of *Dishonored*, the China of *Shanghai Express*, the Hispano-Hollywood of

Devil Is a Woman, has become in *The Shanghai Gesture* a fatal man, and androgyne as well, with the oily and animal face of Victor Mature, so that he may exercise his ravages in a brothel, again suffocating with exoticism. The sumptuous decomposition of a décor runny with byzantinism, asphyxiating us with all it implied of sweat and enervating scents, was perhaps never better "harmonized" than with the circulation of this species of human fauna, whose "rotten grandeur" was once more all baudelairian in essence.

This poetic décor, totally unrealistic and oozing every wretched emanation bewitching the author, whether or not he is steeped in the *Kammerspiel* tradition—we find it all through a work as meticulous in its extravagances as that of Ophuls. Sternberg painted white the sets for *The Case of Lena Smith,* the train in *Shanghai Express,* and the set of the gambling hall of *The Shanghai Gesture.* He made use of the most willfully baroque compositions, limned by a rigorous control of lighting, beginning with his silent films, even the first of which, *The Salvation Hunters,* already expressed his unique mythology. Curtis Harrington reminds us that the America of *The Blonde Venus,* with its low dives, its night clubs, its hotel rooms, its flophouses, which became the archetypes of a whole future of Hollywood cinema, is really strictly Sternbergian, just as is the Peterhof Palace of *The Scarlet Empress.* Sternberg's baroque style sometimes reminds us of Welles's and it is not pure chance that one finds a Goya trait in both men (see *Mr. Arkadin*) as in *The Case of Lena Smith,* in which an amusement park with its distorting mirrors and fantastic tunnels is echoed later in *The Lady of Shanghai.* On the other hand, no cinéaste was ever able to produce from the cadre of the Foreign Legion a dreamlike quality as subtly sophisticated as that of *Morocco,* where the trio, Menjou–Gary Cooper–Marlene, forms a perfect romantic and "decadent" constellation. Here this farrago of a story serves its purpose, as Harrington remarks: to evoke an unusual place, peopled with extraordinary characters thrown into adventures as melodramatic as they are erotic.

This is doubtless the perspective in which we must view our author's silent films: *The Salvation Hunters,* Sternberg's first film, is the one in which he expresses naive confidence in the interior redemption of the most dejected souls despite their nightmarish and putrefied background; *Underworld*, which already bore, unfortunately, the mark of commercial concessions and which was to shape the style and atmosphere of the gangster movies; *The Docks of New York*, a revelation in simplicity. Certainly the psychological study of human wrecks always held his interest. Bancroft, the leader of the gang in *Underworld*, was the vindicator who saved a prostitute from suicide, then married her in an atmosphere of picaresque lyricism that reminds us at once of Pabst and Borzage. But it was really the taste for dank interiors, for musty and acrid smells, drenched textures, and the search for moments when truth blends with bad dreams—the night in the port, the bunker-hands in the stokeholes, the pathetic and derisory wedding before an improvised altar—that was the object of his aesthetic interest.

But this atmosphere, no more than in *The Shanghai Gesture*, is not simply virtuosity. For Sternberg, it has to reveal an inexorable festering of fatality. The tradition of the *Kammerspiel* is not far removed. Later on, it will limn Marlene's face without neglecting the décor that he will illumine with his strange emanations. In this respect, Sternberg's masterpiece—at least his most famous work—remains *The Blue Angel*. Let us not look for the delineation of a certain social reality that crumbles under the author's satire, as in Heinrich Mann. From now on, however, he will affirm the demolition of that aesthetic, the unnameable work of Time fused with the proliferation of a spiritual cancer inside a brain and a society. Here is not only the paroxysm of expressionism but above all the false exorcism of one obsessed and already a prisoner of his morass. *The Blue Angel* was almost insupportable in its excesses, extending the limits of bad taste (which some scenes of *The Shanghai Gesture* will extend even further), emphasizing the sensuous spell of that Germany whose vulgar fascination was embodied in Marlene Dietrich's costumes in it. Epic of filth and abjection, this film is undoubtedly a clinical document, a case-history like the Marlene series that is to follow.

Every cinéaste is haunted by an obsession. Sternberg's is desire, so obvious from one of his most recent works, *Anatahan*. In June of 1944, a group of Japanese military was stranded by an air attack on their convoy on the island of Anatahan and lived there for seven years on the margin of the war.

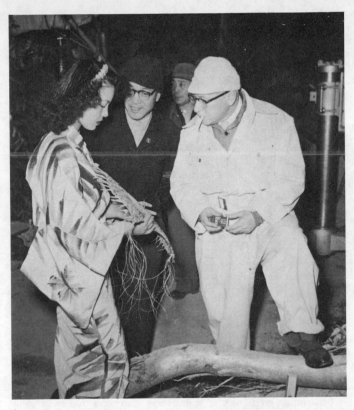

Two years later Sternberg is invited to Japan to make a film and given "carte blanche" and complete autonomy one last time. The result is *Anatahan*, a bizarre postscript to the late war in the Pacific. He discovers in Tokyo a "Japanese Dietrich"—Akemi Negishi—seen here on the set with him and the interpreter. (1953)

Anatahan turns out to be his most personal work, as much a study in behaviorism on a universal scale as a retelling of a true and violent anecdote about some shipwrecked Japanese sailors stranded on a jungle isle. A narration written and spoken by the director gives the film that rarest quality—a fourth dimension. Sternberg's last film. (1953)

Sternberg imagined * that this island was inhabited by a young and seductive woman whose very presence will mean provocation and murder to the stranded men. There no longer will be soldiers or friends, but primitive man, whom forced confinement suddenly confronts with his own demons, obscure forces that rule and submerge him. Stroheim's and Buñuel's names were mentioned in connection with this film. But a beautiful theme is not enough: the essential is to know whether Sternberg was really able to master it. Such was not the opinion of Lotte Eisner, who was dismayed by this "bric-a-brac of bazaar eroticism." There may be reasons to argue about the unrealistic style and certain insistent expressions, but we cannot negate the heart-rending seriousness and autobiographical significance of the film, as testified by a commentary written and read by the director himself. As a result, according to Philippe Demonsablon's trenchant observation, "The account becomes a horrible and necessary ceremony that gives reality to the words of the one who gives the account." *Anatahan* thus appears as the result of a meditation directed toward woman and love, a last exorcism of eroticism, the very ambiguity of which accounts for its savor. "I cultivated my hysteria with delight," wrote Baudelaire. Is Sternberg a modern or a decadent patrician? Perhaps this cinéaste was lacking just that which the author of *Les Fleurs du Mal* possessed: an intelligence and a willpower strong enough to discover beyond his nerves a "new thrill" that was not just a spasm and convulsion.

Les Grandes Cinéastes, Éditions Universitaires, 1959.

Michael Aubriant

And here once more is *The Blue Angel*, not in any of those ciné-clubs, to impress the *aficionados*, but on view in two Paris theatres, as a regular show, as if this film had been made yesterday. I was trembling when I bought my ticket, less afraid for Sternberg, whose glory never stops growing, or

* The principal ingredients of the plot of *Anatahan* were not imagined by Sternberg but were based on actual fact, reported in the press—including the woman. (Ed. Note)

Jannings, that pachyderm ham, but for Marlene, the Marlene whose picture we used to pin inside our school books.

She has changed a great deal and the film along with her. It no longer tells us the exact same story. We probably all were victims of an illusion, the cinema historians above all. What is *The Blue Angel?* The adventure of an honorable high-school professor whom a trollop performing in some deadfall reduces to a crawling worm? Jannings damning himself for a Marlene who incarnates all sensuality, perversity, and female trickery? This is not at all certain.

Compared to today's amazons, the Marlene we rediscover is candor personified; a good-hearted little trouper, a bit overly romantic, perhaps, flattered by the attentions of a pedant old enough to be her papa, dragging him along for four years like a ball and chain, flattered to have been chosen by that solemn ninny. Not a trace of malice. She prefers this clod to her gilded coxcombs. Of course she ends up cuckolding him, but almost against her own will. The idiot dies from it. Good riddance!

A pretty gretchen, cutely set on her sturdy peasant legs, more touching than sensual and more disquieting, in fact, with her alluring lace panties attracting passing sailors and provincial schoolboys, set ablaze by a bit of naked thigh, with her broken little voice of a honky-tonk singer, whom the first ruffian can buy for a bottle of champagne. All this, seen at this distance, now appears like a sad farce, a satire half-ferocious, half-tender, typical of a certain kind of German sentimentality, of a certain German taste for tinsel, exuberance, and misery.

It is not certain that Sternberg, under the impression that he was making a German *Nana*, was fully aware of this. No doubt he was the first victim of the myth he had created, chained to Marlene, polishing her from film to film to transform her into a diaphanous idol with a laquered face who soon would no longer need her Pygmalion.

France-Soir—Paris Presse
January 20, 1966.

Jean de Baroncelli

A FORMIDABLE VOICE

Sure, Marlene is there in a role tailored to her measure.
We see her as a frightened young girl, her face smooth and
candid, little by little metamorphosized into a redoubtable
woman who will reign under the name of Catherine II of Russia. Loving, hating, revolted, jilted, and triumphant, she
hardly ever leaves the screen. And we wait for her and we
spy on her because she is so famous. But fascination is no
longer a part of the game, time has passed, the myth has
turned into a memory. As Catherine, Marlene is but an
actress, an excellent actress, like many others . . .

That which attracts us, which puts us under a spell, however, which stupefies us (and helps us forget that somewhat
absurd gallop up the palace steps)* is another presence, an
invisible one, but much more obsessive than the first one. It
is a formidable voice. It is Sternberg in person.

He said it in his book, he did it all by himself. "With
one exception, the story, the décor, the settings, the sculptures, the costumes, the photography, all were mine." Prodigious pride, the morbid jealousy of an artist? Perhaps. But
mainly an irresistible need to create and to carry alone the
weight of his creation. *The Scarlet Empress* is, in fact, a pure
artistic creation, a visual symphony, based on the triple theme
of ambition, voluptuousness, and death, an unfurling of
images whose freedom of design reminds one at moments of
the silent film, a baroque frenzy of flesh and marble monsters
that leads us straight into this "universe," to which Sternberg dreamed of attracting crowds.

It is unnecessary to evoke Flaubert with his famous
"*Madame Bovary, c'est moi.*" We don't doubt for a moment
that the real "scarlet empress" is not that blonde shadow
agitating the screen. The Hollywood people were right:
Josef von Sternberg just made his own portrait! but they

* At the Sandhurst military academy in England, there is a tra-
ditional ritual calling for an officer to gallop his horse up the steps
of the grand entrance through the doorway, following the passing-
out parade. (Ed. Note)

don't know—besides, it does not matter to them—that without dreamers and egocentrics of that kind art would never flower.

Le Monde, March 2, 1966.

Michel Cournot

A DREAM "CINEMATIQUE"

The Scarlet Empress, the story of which is, in a way, the youth of Catherine the Great up to her ascension to the throne, is, to its smallest detail, the work of one man. Sternberg wrote the story and dialogue, suggested the décor and the ikons, designed the statues—which are more numerous in the film than the actors—sketched the costumes, arranged the lights, composed some of the music and personally directed the Los Angeles Philharmonic Orchestra which plays the score.

That basic fundamental of cinema, movement, was approached by Sternberg in *The Scarlet Empress*, paradoxically enough, through his immobile chimeras: the statues. The very first scene foretells these statues through a doll that the future empress, still a child, holds in her arms. Let us note here that when the Czar Peter is suddenly awakened the night of his assassination, he holds another doll-like figure in his sleep: one of the toy wooden soldiers he used to drop all over the palace.

Reduced in size or gigantic, but often of the same size as the actors, this crowd of statues, tortured or placid, twisted or straight, constantly help or disturb the living action of the film. The characters cannot sit down, they can only lie down against, next to, and even inside the statues. They must go around them to move. The statues are erect when characters prostrate themselves, or they lie prostrate when the characters themselves are erect.

Obviously condemned, these statufied beings have a part in the events: they observe a world forbidden to them, they spy on it, defy it, are resigned to it, indifferent to it, they disapprove of it, they refuse to have anything to do with it, they sometimes become human, incredibly they even change their poses, according to the inflections of the film, so much so that eventually their presence, with all its intentions and judgments, far exceeds that of the living protagonists, the historical personages, the actors.

Constantly judged by these mute presences, as insinuating as they are stubborn, what can the players do? They can "play," which is to say *"they can proceed with the reconstitution of motives which are the cause of their actions and their words."* But *"the cinema is only a highly developed theatre of shadows, and wishing to manipulate humans as if they were puppets is to get into trouble.*[*] It seems that every personage of *The Scarlet Empress* spontaneously finds his way toward animation as if it were a reaction, or a reference, to the anti-cinema accusation of the motionless statues. Czar Peter and Sam Jaffe, who portrays him, decompose several motionless "moments" into an animation, broken and cut, which is that of automatons: Sam Jaffe never connects his gestures, he goes from one prostration to another prostration, he seems to leap over life. The Master of the Hounds, and John Lodge, who plays him (after this picture Lodge became Congressman, Governor of Connecticut, and United States Ambassador to Spain), get into a false situation, an affected, behavior-mimicking impassability. As for Catherine, Marlene Deitrich is the only one whose guileless transports sometimes escape the clutches of the statues, because of her vital life force, and yet, when Marlene Dietrich, too, stands completely still, Sternberg lingers and strolls over her fabulous face with his lens as if he were traversing a beach in the morning (*"the forehead is a fragment of the sky, the hair are clouds"*).[†] When she, too, is paralyzed like an object, her presence succeeds in overwhelming, though not without a struggle, the demonic presence of the sculptured monsters that engulf her.

It is quite certain that each tenth of a second in the film, each aspect of immobility or of movement, has in addition a precise significance, a responsibility to the events described and the spirits evoked, and the expressions of the statues change as much as those of the actors. If for once one wishes to watch a living mediation regarding one of the mysteries of cinema, movement, one must look straight at those statues and those

[*] These quotations are from Sternberg's autobiography, *Fun in a Chinese Laundry.* (New York: The Macmillan Co., 1965)
 [†] Ibid.

actors, and observe how the moving image modifies the meaning of the inanimate one and in what way.

On the studio set, statues and players stand in space, whereas the white screen is flat: here is another simple cinema element upon which Sternberg now acts, by animating other images, the innumerable paintings and ikons which cover the walls, the pillars, the doors, the sleighs, the bells, the backs of mirrors, everything. He sometimes makes these flat images of the paintings move in such a hallucinatory way that the screen itself seems to "turn on its hinges," and it is the screen itself that looks when Peter, to spy on his wife, drills a hole into the eye of a saint who is, incidentally, armed with a large knife. The paintings are as flat as the screen, but the image of cinema remains, here as everywhere else, *"restive and trembling with emotion."* It is when the paintings take over the relay from the statues that Sternberg *"mingles the real and the imaginary until the spectator is confounded."* He also intermingles them with incredible audacity as when, to show for the first time the Russia of the peasants, he superimposes on the slow traveling shots of models in relief and flat ikons lightninglike flashes of white cavalry, against the sombre background, charging across the screen.

Between the reliefs of both statues and actors flattened on the screen, and the flat of the ikons to which the movement of the camera gives imaginary perspectives, Sternberg leads a game of make-believe that is a breath of cinema in a rough stage. This same obsession of the spirit also gives us that frenzy characterized by his filming of doors. *The Scarlet Empress* is an organized nightmare of doors, also foretold in the first sequence, even before Catherine's doll, when the shadow of who knows what dead tree appears on the open door of the little girl's room. What can one say about the painted doors in Peter's palace, doors a hundred times as large as the characters, the tops of which one never sees, elaborately decorated doors, the opening and closing of which each time seem to demand momentarily insoluble problems and superhuman efforts?

The eyes rest on another door, less noticeable, the door behind a mirror, or by chance behind the mirror of the Empress's bedroom, the secret door through which come and go the lovers for a night. A simple wooden door, rather small this one, half-lost in the dark, and on which one nevertheless sees the shadow of a monster statue with horns and vampire wings, a surface of mystery and lies, a sombre screen on which shines only the golden chimera of a handle. It looks as though this cinema screen, which we are so used to, is entirely occupied by the motionless and dimly lit surface of this simple door; it is then we immediately plunge into an abyss of dreams from whose depths *"the sighs of the queen and the cries of the fairy-queen"* of Nerval begin to fill the universe.

Two well known sequences of *The Scarlet Empress* are among the strongest of the cinema.

The first is a single shot. The camera plunges down onto the table set for a wedding feast. We advance slowly along this table. As our gaze glides along, we see statues of naked women, peelings, melted candles, cadavers of animals, wigs, horns, a soup simmering like a witch's brew, feathers, a crown, fruit. There is a disorder of blacks and whites, which is the disorder of objects "naturally" to be found on a festive table at the court of Imperial Russia but we move further into this nightmare, into this hallucinating landscape of injustices and tortures. The camera, having slowly reached the end of the table, now rises almost imperceptibly and moves slowly back. This time, each side of the table, we see the guests, seated between the gargoyle-statues, almost motionless, absolutely silent, the living are dead, one hears only the faint sound of a violin playing a gypsy tune. Nothing has been said and yet, with a single shot, through the magic of the cinema, all has been said about the palaces of the Czars. It is the summit of art.

The second is the marriage of Catherine and Peter at the Cathedral of Kazan. This sequence is filmed in 29 shots that require the special attention of the spectators, particularly shots 15, 17, 19, and 22, which are close-ups of Marlene Dietrich and of a candle behind a veil, as well as close-up 27, of the hands of the betrothed pair. I know Russia and it seems to me that all the poetry of an ancient country is there. One cannot help admiring also shots 1 and 28 which describe the same path in space, but reversed, penetrating and surrounding the total ensemble of the scene. Yes, the sequence on Kazan, alone, is a monument. To evoke the Russia of another time, Eisenstein did something else, but he did not do better.

A last word regarding the sound track of *The Scarlet Em-*

The author has a reunion with his two subjects at a party celebrating the gala opening of the Dietrich Retrospective at the Museum of Modern Art in New York. (1957) *Photo: Fred Stein*

press. It is one of the most beautiful ever made. Viennese music, mad circus music, which accentuates the madness of the costumes and coiffures that encrust the unreality of operetta in the pages of sinister history. The rest is silence, except for some fleeting sounds, a necklace torn off, a hay stalk crushed, a breath, the turning of a lock, the taffeta of a dress that rustles like leaves in the wind. False music and a dozen sudden starts of sound accompany, as in the empty beyond, these apparitions of phantoms whose images and sounds are confounded. Sternberg superbly makes a lie out of the beautiful words he quotes from Bela Balazs: "Sound does not project a shadow." One can say that *The Scarlet Empress* brings to its highest degree of expressiveness *"the search for obscure values, the orderly investigation of chaos, and the compression in a limited space of an infinite spiritual power."* It is to this unforgettable sound track created by Sternberg that we owe the final sequence, that unleashing of the hordes of black and white horses, galloping through the corridors, the salons, the council rooms, up to the throne . . . stamping through the courtyards and up the palace steps in an immense thunderous noise which consummates this masterpiece against the salvos of revolt and the drums of death.

Le Nouvel Observateur, February 23, 1966.
230 *Herman G. Weinberg*

L'ENVOI

Mysterious of profile, implacable of visage, his genius measures up to his obsessions. Even those who question his concepts cannot help admitting the quasi-hypnotic trance in which his films engulf them. It is hard to tell who vanquished him, Marlene or Hollywood. But, in fact, is he really vanquished? After a period of silence, he produced his strangest and most fascinating work, *The Shanghai Gesture*. . . . Is it possible that one day, eluding the attention of his jailers, he will transport us anew into that kingdom of his dreams, into that hell of his nightmares? For to them he is a menace as to us he is a promise.

Cahiers du Cinéma, Paris
Noël, 1955

Filmography

"Where is this division of labor to end and what object does it finally serve? No doubt another may also think for me, but it is not therefore desirable that he should do so to the exclusion of my thinking for myself."

—THOREAU

(Screen credits that appear on a film can often be a matter of company policy and/or contractual obligation. The following credits are not in every case those which appeared on the screen, but they represent the true credits, according to Von Sternberg.)

In 1924 Sternberg acted as scenarist, photographer, and assistant director on *By Divine Right,** a P.R.C. film for F.B.O., directed by Roy William Neill starring Elliot Dexter and Anna Q. Nilsson. That same year he directed his first scene, in the same company's *Vanity's Price*, for which Neill was also the director, an adaptation of Gertrude Atherton's novel *Black Oxen*, again with Anna Q. Nilsson. The scene, of a rejuvenation operation, became famous, even after the film was forgotten. It marked Sternberg's debut as a director. "A long journey," said Lao Tse, "begins with a single step."

1925

THE SALVATION HUNTERS

Original scenario by Josef von Sternberg.
Photography: Edward Gheller. A Josef von Sternberg production released by Academy Pictures and distributed by United Artists.
Première: February 15, 1925

* It was in this film that Sternberg discovered Georgia Hale as an extra. She was subsequently to become his first female star.

Players: George K. Arthur (The boy), Georgia Hale (The girl), Bruce Guerin (The child), Otto Matiesen (The man), Nellie Bly Baker (The woman), Olaf Hytten (The brute), Stuart Holmes (The gentleman).

THE EXQUISITE SINNER

Scenario: Josef von Sternberg and Alice Deuer Miller, from the novel, *Escape*, by Alden Brooks. *Assistant:* Robert Florey. *Photography:* Maximilian Fabian. *Distributed by* Metro-Goldwyn-Mayer. *Première:* March 28, 1926.

Players: Conrad Nagel (Dominique Prad), Renée Adorée (Gypsy girl), George K. Arthur (Captain's orderly), Paulette Duval (Yvonne), Frank Currier (Captain), Matthew Betz (Gypsy chief), Helene d'Algy and Claire Dubrey (Dominique's sisters), Myrna Loy ("Living Statue").

This film was remade by Phil Rosen for MGM and therefore was not recognized in its released version by Sternberg.

THE MASKED BRIDE (Abandoned)

Scenario: Carey Wilson, after a novel by Leon Abrams. *Photography:* Oliver Marsh. *Assistant:* Robert Florey. *Distributed by* Metro-Goldwyn-Mayer. *Première:* December 13, 1925.

This film was quickly left unfinished by Sternberg, the major part of it being completed by W. Christy Cabanne for MGM.

Projects: A project for Mary Pickford, *Backwash*. Not realized.

1926

THE SEA GULL (WOMAN OF THE SEA) Unreleased.

Original scenario by Josef von Sternberg.
Photography: Paul Ivano. *Settings:* Danny Hall. *Produced by* Charles Chaplin.

Players: Edna Purviance, Eve Sothern, Gane Whitman.

A simple love story served as the basis for this film, in which the changing patterns of the sea were used for psychological and atmospheric underscoring of the action, which was photographed largely on the sea coast of Monterey, California. The film was previewed only once in Beverly Hills, after which Chaplin decided, for reasons of his own, not to release it. In the late Twenties, John Grierson, one of the few people who saw it, called it, "The most beautiful film ever shot in Hollywood."

In 1927, Sternberg directed the final scenes of Clara Bow's hit, *It*, from the novel by Elinor Glyn, when its director, Clarence Badger, was unable to finish his work. (For Paramount.)

The same year he served in a similar capacity on Frank Lloyd's *Children of Divorce*, starring Esther Ralston, Gary Cooper, and Clara Bow. (For Paramount.)

1927

UNDERWORLD

Original idea: Ben Hecht. *Scenario:* Josef von Sternberg.
Photography: Bert Glennon. *Settings:* Hans Dreier.
Distributed by: Paramount. *Première:* September 3, 1927.

Players: Clive Brook ("Rolls Royce"), Evelyn Brent ("Feathers" McCoy), George Bancroft ("Bull" Weed), Larry Semon ("Slippery" Lewis), Fred Kohler (Buck Mulligan), Helen Lynch (Mulligan's girl), Jerry Mandy (Paloma).

1928

THE LAST COMMAND

Original scenario: Josef von Sternberg, based on an idea told to Sternberg by Ernst Lubitsch.
Photography: Bert Glennon. *Settings:* Hans Dreier.
Distributed by: Paramount. *Première:* January 23, 1928.

Players: Emil Jannings (Grand Duke Sergius Alexander), Evelyn Brent (Natasha Dobrowa), William Powell (Leo

Andreiev), Nicholas Soussanin (Adjutant), Jack Raymond (Assistant Director), Michael Visaroff (Valet).

The Street of Sin, an original scenario by Sternberg for Emil Jannings, whose direction was begun by Mauritz Stiller, continued by Lothar Mendes, and finished by Ludwig Berger for Paramount. With Fay Wray and Olga Baclanova. The setting was London's Soho district. *Subject:* The Salvation Army.

At the request of Paramount and with the approval of Stroheim, Sternberg recut the latter's *The Wedding March*, to reduce its length. Paramount subsequently divided Sternberg's version into two parts (the second was called: *The Honeymoon*). Part One was released for its première October 6, 1928. The second part was never shown in the United States.

THE DRAGNET

Original story: "Night Stick" by Oliver H.P. Garrett.
Scenario: Jules Furthman. *Photography:* Harold Rosson.
Settings: Hans Dreier. *Distributed by:* Paramount. *Première* May 26, 1928.

Players: George Bancroft ("Two Gun" Nolan), Evelyn Brent ("The Magpie"), William Powell ("Dapper" Frank Trent), Fred Kohler ("Gabby" Steve), Francis McDonald ("Sniper" Dawson), Leslie Fenton (Donovan).

THE DOCKS OF NEW YORK

Original scenario: Jules Furthman, suggested by "The Dock Walloper" by John Monk Saunders. *Photography:* Harold Rosson. *Settings:* Hans Dreier. *Distributed by:* Paramount. *Première:* September 29, 1928.

Players: George Bancroft (Bill Roberts, the stevedore), Betty Compson (Sadie), Olga Baclanova (Lou), Clyde Cook ("Sugar" Steve), Mitchell Lewis (Third Engineer), Gustav von Seyffertitz ("Hymn Book" Harry), Lillian Worth (Steve's girl).

1929

THE CASE OF LENA SMITH

Original scenario: Josef von Sternberg.
Photography: Harold Rosson. *Settings:* Hans Dreier.
Distributed by: Paramount. *Première:* January 19, 1929.

Players: Esther Ralston (Lena Smith), James Hall (Franz Hofrat), Gustav von Seyffertitz (Herr Hofrat), Emily Fitzroy (Frau Hofrat), Fred Kohler (Stefan), Betty Aho (Stefan's sister), Lawrence Grant (Commissioner), Alex Woloshin (Janitor), Ann Brody (Janitor's wife).

THUNDERBOLT *

Original story: Jules and Charles Furthman.
Scenario: Josef von Sternberg. *Photography:* Henry Gerrard.
Settings: Hans Dreier. *Distributed by:* Paramount.
Première: June 22, 1929.

Players: George Bancroft ("Thunderbolt"), Richard Arlen (Bob Morgan), Fay Wray ("Ritzy"), Tully Marshall (Warden), Eugenie Besserer (Mrs. Moran), James Spottswood ("Snapper" O'Shea), Fred Kohler ("Bad Al" Frieberg), Mike Donlin ("Kentucky" Sampson), S. S. Stewart (Negro convict), George Irving (Bank officer), Robert Elliott (Priest), William Thorne (Police inspector), E. H. Calvert (District Attorney).

1930

THE BLUE ANGEL

Scenario: Josef von Sternberg, freely adapted by him from the novel, *Professor Unrat*, by Heinrich Mann.
Photography: Gunther Rittau, Hans Schneeberger.
Settings: Otto Hunte, Emil Hasler.
Lyrics and songs: Friedrich Hollander.

* Von Sternberg's first sound film. There was no musical background.

Produced by: Erich Pommer for Ufa, Berlin, and produced in two versions, German and English.
Distributed by: Paramount (U.S.).
Première: January 3, 1931.
Berlin Première: April 1, 1930.

Players: Emil Jannings (Prof. Immanuel Rat), Marlene Dietrich (Lola Froehlich), Kurt Gerron (Kiepert, a magician), Rosa Valetti (Guste, his wife), Hans Albers (Mazeppa), Eduard von Winterstein (Principal of the school), Reinhold Bernt (The clown), Hans Roth (The beadle), Rolf Mueller, Roland Varno, Karl Balhaus, Robert Klein-Loerk (students), Karl Huszar-Puffy (The publican), Wilhelm Diegelmann (Captain), Gerhard Bienert (Policeman), Ilse Fürstenberg (Rat's housekeeper).

Four songs: "Nimm Dich in acht vor blonden Frauen," "Ich bin von Kopf bis Fuss auf Liebe eingestellt," "Ich bin die fesche Lola," "Kinder, heut' abend such' ich mir was aus."

MOROCCO

Scenario: Josef von Sternberg, based on the novel *Amy Jolly*, by Benno Vigny.
Photography: Lee Garmes and Lucien Ballard.
Settings: Hans Dreier.
Songs: "Give Me the Man Who Does Things" and "What Am I Bid for My Apples?" by Leo Robin (lyrics) and Karl Hajos (music). "Quand l'Amour Meurt" by Millandy and Cremieux.
Distributed by: Paramount. *Première:* December 6, 1930.

Players: Gary Cooper (Legionnaire Tom Brown), Marlene Dietrich (Amy Jolly), Adolphe Menjou (LeBessière), Ullrich Haupt (Adjutant Caesar), Juliette Compton (Anna Dolores), Francis MacDonald (Corporal Tatoche), Albert Conti (Col. Quinnevières), Eve Sothern (Mme. Caesar), Paul Porcasi (Impresario, Lo Tinto), Émile Chautard (French General), Michael Visaroff.

1931

DISHONORED

Original scenario: Josef von Sternberg.
Photography: Lee Garmes. *Settings:* Hans Dreier.
Distributed by: Paramount. *Première:* April 4, 1931.

Players: Marlene Dietrich (X-27), Victor McLaglen (Lt. Kranau), Lew Cody (Col. Kovrin), Gustav von Seyffertitz (Austrian Secret Service Head), Warner Oland (Capt. von Hindau), Barry Norton (Young Lieutenant), Davison Clark (Court Martial presiding officer), Wilfred Lucas (General Dymov).

Music: Ivanovici's "Danube Waves," Beethoven's "Moonlight Sonata," and original music by Sternberg.

AN AMERICAN TRAGEDY

From the novel by Theodore Dreiser. *Adaptation:* Josef von Sternberg and Samuel Hoffenstein.
Scenario: Josef von Sternberg.
Photography: Lee Garmes. *Settings:* Hans Dreier.
Distributed by: Paramount. *Première:* August 22, 1931.

Players: Phillips Holmes (Clyde Griffiths), Sylvia Sidney (Roberta Alden), Frances Dee (Sondra Finchley), Irving Pichel (Orville Mason), Frederick Burton (Samuel Griffiths), Claire McDowell (Mrs. Samuel Griffiths), Wallace Middleton (Gilbert Griffiths), Vivian Winston (Myra Griffiths), Emmett Corrigan (Belknap), Lucille La Verne (Mrs. Asa Griffiths), Charles B. Middleton (Jephson), Albert Hart (Titus Alden), Fanny Midgely (Mrs. Alden), Arline Judge (Bella Griffiths), Evelyn Pierce (Bertine Cranston), Arnold Korff (Judge), Elizabeth Forrester (Jill Trumbell), Russell Powell (Coroner), Imboden Parrish (Earl Newcomb), Richard Kramer (Deputy Sheriff).

1932

SHANGHAI EXPRESS

Scenario: Josef von Sternberg and Jules Furthman. From a story idea by Harry Hervey.
Photography: Lee Garmes. *Settings:* Hans Dreier.
Distributed by: Paramount. *Première:* February 12, 1932.

Players: Marlene Dietrich (Shanghai Lily), Clive Brook (Capt. Donald Harvey), Anna May Wong (Hui Fei), Warner Oland (Henry Chang), Eugene Pallette (Sam Salt), Lawrence Grant (Mr. Carmichael), Louise Closser Hale (Mrs. Haggerty), Gustav von Seyffertitz (Eric Baum), Émile Chautard (Maj. Lenard).

THE BLONDE VENUS

Original scenario: Josef von Sternberg.
Photography: Bert Glennon. *Settings:* Wiard Ihnen.
Songs: "Hot Voodoo" and "You Little So and So" by Sam Coslow and Ralph Rainger; "I Could Be Annoyed" by Leo Robin and Dick Whiting.
Distributed by: Paramount. *Première:* Sept. 16, 1932.

Players: Marlene Dietrich (Helen Faraday), Herbert Marshall (Edward Faraday), Cary Grant (Nick Townsend), Dickie Moore (Johnny Faraday), Gene Morgan (Ben Smith), Rita La Roy ("Taxi Belle" Hooper), Robert Emmett O'Connor (Dan O'Connor), Hattie McDaniel (Negro maid), Sidney Toler (Detective Wilson).

In November, 1932, Sternberg and his cameraman of *The Sea Gull,* Paul Ivano, went to the Caribbean to shoot scenes of a hurricane for a projected circus story by Miss Dietrich. The hurricane failed to materialize and they returned to Hollywood with the project abandoned.

1934

THE SCARLET EMPRESS

Scenario: Josef von Sternberg, based on a diary of Catherine the Great.
Photography: Bert Glennon. *Settings:* Hans Dreier, Peter Balbusch, Richard Kollorsz.
Music: From Tchaikovsky, Mendelssohn, and Wagner, arranged by John M. Leipold and W. Frank Harling.
Distributed by: Paramount. *Première:* September 7, 1934.

Players: Marlene Dietrich (Sophia Frederika, later Catherine II), John Lodge (Duke Alexei), Sam Jaffe (Grand Duke Peter), Louise Dresser (Empress Elizabeth), Maria Sieber (Catherine as a child), C. Aubrey Smith (Prince August), Ruthelma Stevens (Countess Elizabeth), Olive Tell (Princess Johanna), Gavin Gordon (Gregory Orloff), Jameson Thomas (Lt. Ovtsya), Hans von Twardowski (Ivan Shuvolov), Davison Clark (Archmandrite and Arch Episcope Simeon Tevedovsky).

1935

THE DEVIL IS A WOMAN

Scenario and adaptation: Josef von Sternberg, after the novel *Woman and Puppet*, by Pierre Louys.
Photography: Josef von Sternberg, assisted by Lucien Ballard. *Settings:* Hans Dreier and Sternberg. *Music:* Arranged by Ralph Rainger and Andrea Setaro, from Rimsky-Korsakov's "Caprice Espagnole" and Spanish folk-songs. *Song:* "Three Sweethearts Have I" by Leo Robin and Ralph Rainger.
Distributed by: Paramount. *Première:* May 3, 1935.

Players: Marlene Dietrich (Concha Perez), Lionel Atwill (Don Pasqual), Cesar Romero (Antonio Galvan), Edward Everett Horton (Don Paquito), Alison Skipworth (Señora Perez), Don Alvarado (Morenito), Morgan Wallace (Dr. Mendez), Tempe Pigott (Tuerta), Jill Dennett (Maria), Lawrence Grant (Conductor), Charles Sellon (Letter writer),

Luisa Espinal (Gypsy dancer), Hank Mann (Foreman, snow-bound train), Edwin Maxwell (Superintendent, tobacco factory).

Prize at the Venice Film Festival, 1935, for the best photography.

CRIME AND PUNISHMENT

Scenario: S. K. Lauren and Joseph Anthony, after the novel by Fyodor Dostoievski.
Photography: Lucien Ballard. *Settings*: Stephen Goossens.
Costumes: Murray Mayer. *Music*: Louis Silver.
Edited: Richard Calhoon. *Produced by*: B. P. Schulberg.
Distributed by: Columbia. *Première*: November 20, 1935.

Players: Peter Lorre (Raskolnikov), Edward Arnold (Inspector Porfiry), Marian Marsh (Sonya), Tala Birell (Antonya), Elizabeth Risdon (Mrs. Raskolnikov), Robert Allen (Dmitri), Douglas Dumbrille (Grilov), Gene Lockhart (Lushin), Charles Waldron (University Rector), Thurston Hall (Editor), Johnny Arthur (Clerk), Mrs. Patrick Campbell (Pawnbroker), Rafaelo Ottiano (Landlady), Michael Mark (Painter prisoner).

1936

THE KING STEPS OUT

Scenario: Sidney Buchman, from the operetta *Cissy*, by Herbert and Ernst Marischka, with music by Fritz Kreisler.
Assistant director: Wilhelm Thiele.
Photography: Lucien Ballard. *Settings*: Stephen Goossens.
Ballet: Albertina Rasch. *Costumes*: Ernst Dryden.
Music: Arranged by Howard Jackson, from themes by Fritz Kreisler.
Distributed by: Columbia. *Première*: May 15, 1936.

Players: Grace Moore (Cissy, afterwards Empress Elizabeth), Franchot Tone (Franz Josef, afterwards Emperor), Walter Connolly (Maximilian), Raymond Walburn (von Kempen), Victor Jory (Palfi), Elizabeth Risden (Sofia), Nana Bryant (Louise), Frieda Inescourt (Helena), Thurston Hall (Major),

Herman Bing (Pretzelberger), George Hassell (Herlicka), John Arthur (Chief of Secret Police).

1937

I, CLAUDIUS (Unfinished)

Scenario: Josef von Sternberg, based on the historical novel *I, Claudius*, by Robert Graves. *Photography:* Georges Périnal. *Settings:* Vincent Korda. *Costumes:* John Armstrong. *Choreography:* Agnes de Mille. *Produced by:* Alexander Korda for London Films.

Players: Charles Laughton (Tiberius Claudius Drusus), Merle Oberon (Messalina), Flora Robson (Livia, Empress Dowager, mother of Claudius), Emlyn Williams (Caligula), Robert Newton, Ralph Richardson, John Clements, Basil Gill, Everley Gregg.

Sternberg's difficulties in handling Laughton, who had suddenly developed some eccentricities, and an automobile accident injury sustained by Merle Oberon, brought production to a halt early in the film. Some 20 minutes of edited footage of several scenes remain in the collection of the National Film Archives in London and have been incorporated into the BBC television film, *The Epic That Never Was*, recounting via interviews with some the principals involved, including the director, the reasons for the curtailment of this ambitious project.

Other projects: Germinal, from the Zola novel, of which a treatment exists. To have starred Jean-Louis Barrault and Hilde Krahl. The director's illness put a halt to this. Pirandello's *Six Characters in Search of an Author*, with Max Reinhardt playing the stage manager, was another unfulfilled project. Also unrealized was the plan to film *Austrian Peasant Wedding*, after a ballet, in Austria. An abortive attempt to direct Hedy Lamarr (October, 1938) in a film, *New York Cinderella*, from a story by Charles MacArthur, followed, but after 18 days Sternberg gave up and Frank Borzage took over. The picture was not released however until two years later when W. S. Van Dyke re-shot it. Under its new title, *I Take*

This Woman, and with Spencer Tracy and Laraine Day also in the cast, MGM finally launched it to a disastrous press. While at MGM Sternberg added some touches to its big Johann Strauss film, *The Great Waltz*, which Julien Duvivier had directed, and remained just long enough to complete his contract at the studio with the perfunctory *Sergeant Madden*.

1939

SERGEANT MADDEN

Scenario: Wells Root, from the story "A Gun in His Hand," by William A. Ulman.
Photography: John Seitz. *Settings*: Cedric Gibbons, Randall Duell. *Special effects*: Peter Balbusch.
Music: William Axt. *Distributed by*: Metro-Goldwyn-Mayer. *Première*: March 24, 1939.

Players: Wallace Beery (Sean Madden), Tom Brown (Al Boylan, Jr.), Alan Curtis (Dennis Madden), Laraine Day (Eileen Daly), Fay Holden (Mary Madden), Marc Lawrence ("Piggy" Ceders), Marian Martin (Charlotte), David Gorcey ("Punchy").

1941

THE SHANGHAI GESTURE

Scenario: Josef von Sternberg, adapted from the play by John Colton.
Photography: Paul Ivano. *Settings*: Boris Leven, Howard Bristol. *Murals*: Keye Luke. *Music*: Richard Hageman. *Miss Munson's costumes*: Royer. *Miss Tierney's costumes*: Oleg Cassini. *Produced by*: Arnold Pressburger. *Distributed by*: United Artists. *Première*: February 6, 1942.

Players: Gene Tierney ("Poppy"–Victoria Charteris), Walter Huston (Sir Guy Charteris), Victor Mature (Doctor Omar), Ona Munson ("Mother Gin Sling"), Phyllis Brooks (Dixie Pomeroy), Albert Basserman (Commissioner), Maria Ouspenskaya (Amah), Eric Blore (Bookkeeper), Ivan Lebedeff

(Gambler), Mike Mazurki (Coolie), Clyde Fillmore (Comprador), Rex Evans (Counsellor Brooks), Grayce Hampton (Socialite), Micharl Delmatoff (Bartender), Marcel Dalio (Croupier), Mikhail Rasumny (Cashier), John Abbott (Poppy's escort).

1943–44

THE TOWN

Scenario: Joseph Krumgold.
Photography: Larry Madison. Philip Dunn in charge of production for the United States Office of War Information.
The town: Madison, Wisconsin.

A one-reel documentary made during World War II to show the many diverse elements that go into the making of a typical American town.

1946

Color consultant for David O. Selznick's *Duel in the Sun.* Sternberg also directed some scenes during a brief illness of the film's director, King Vidor.

Project: The Seven Bad Years (1949) an essay that was to be the prelude to a film examination of the roots of aggressiveness in man that are to be found in his first—formative—seven years "and from which he could extricate himself were he to recognize that an irresponsible child was leading him into trouble." (J.v.S.) No support for this project could be found.

1950

JET PILOT

Scenario, Co-Producer: Jules Furthman.
Photography: Winton C. Hoch. *Aerial photography:* Philip C. Cochran.

Settings: Albert S. D'Agostino and Field Gray.
Music: Bronislaw Kaper.
Costumes: Michael Woulfe.
Edited by: James Wilkinson, Michael McAdam, Harry Marker, William Moore.
Produced by: Howard Hughes.
Distributed by: R.K.O.

Players: Janet Leigh, John Wayne, Hans Conreid, Richard Rober, Paul Fix, Jay C. Flippen, Roland Winters, Ivan Triesault, John Bishop, Perdita Chandler, Joyce Compton.

1951

MACAO

Scenario: Barnard C. Schoenfeld and Stanley Rubin, from a story by Bob Williams.
Photography: Harry J. Wild. *Settings:* Albert S. D'Agostino, Ralph Berger.
Music: Anthony Collins.
Costumes: Michael Woulfe.
Produced by: Howard Hughes. *Co-producer:* Alex Gottlieb.
Associate producer: S. Rubin. *Edited by:* Samuel E. Beetley and Robert Golden.
Distributed by: R.K.O. *Première:* April, 1952.

Players: Jane Russell, Robert Mitchum, William Bendix, Thomas Gomez, Gloria Grahame, Brad Dexter, Edward Ashley, Philip Ahn, Vladimir Sokoloff, Don Zelaya.

Neither *Jet Pilot* nor *Macao* represent authentic works by Von Sternberg, having been so altered for their commercial distribution that little of the director's original intentions was preserved. *Jet Pilot*, for instance, Sternberg's first film in color, retains almost nothing of his experiments in the medium of the color film. As for *Macao*, it was almost entirely re-shot by Nicholas Ray. Of these two films, Sternberg said: "They were for me unsuccessful assignments as the controlling factors were a dozen assorted and constantly shifted producers—never the director—and the only reason I accepted these doubtful conditions was that Howard Hughes promised to give me support and authority for years to come—a promise that was to remain as elusive as he was."

1953

THE SAGA OF ANATAHAN

Scenario: Josef von Sternberg, adapted by him from a book by Michiro Maruyama, based on an actual incident of World War II in the South Pacific reported by *Life* magazine. Narration in English written and spoken by Von Sternberg.
Photography: Josef von Sternberg. *Settings:* Kono.
Music: Akira Ifukube.
Japanese dialogue: Asano.
Produced by: Yoshio Osawa and Nagamasa Kawakita for Daiwa-Towa Productions, Japan.
Première: 1953.

Players: Akemi Negishi, Tadashi Suganuma, Shoji Nakayama, Hiroshi Kondo, Jun Fujikawa, Kisaburo Sawamura, Tadashi Kitagawa, Shozo Miyashita, Rokuriro Kinoya, Dajiro Tamura, Takeshi Suzuki, Shiro Amikura, Kikuji Onoe, Tsuruemu Bando.

Filmed in Kyoto, Japan, in a studio specially built for the film where the sub-tropical island of Anatahan, one of the Marianas group, was reconstructed.

In 1954, Sternberg planned with Gabriel Pascal, in their respective director and producer capacities, to film Shaw's "The Doctor's Dilemma." Not realized.

In 1959, Sternberg acquired an option to film Shelby Foote's novel of a *crime passionel* set in the deep South, *Follow Me Down*. The film was to have been called *The Temptation of Luther Eustus*. Not realized.

· · ·

With the exceptions noted above, Sternberg wrote or supervised the scenarios of all his films and edited them himself. Being himself a cameraman, he also supervised the photography of all his films, determining the angles, lighting, and composition. Two he photographed himself—*The Devil Is a Woman* and *Anatahan*. As to the music, he specified all the sounds, including the music and songs, that were to serve as backgrounds to or source music from the images. Although ideas for sets and costumes were sometimes submitted to him by the set designers and wardrobe people, their essential style was determined by Sternberg. Often they were based on prior fantasies by painters and illustrators of long ago. Just as often, they were products of his own imagination.

Bibliography
(Selective)

I. WRITINGS BY STERNBERG

Books

Daughters of Vienna, a novel, Vienna, 1922. (Translated from the German of Karl Adolph.)

Fun in a Chinese Laundry, an autobiography, Macmillan, 1965. British edition: Secker & Warburg (London), 1966.

Souvenirs d'un montreur d'ombres, French translation of the autobiography, Éditions Robert Laffont (Paris), 1966.

(A German edition of the autobiography, by Friedrich-Verlag [Hanover], is to be published this year.)

Articles

"The Waxen Galatea," *The Director* (Hollywood), 1925. (This was a short story.)

"Come studio i mei film," *Cinema* (Rome), No. 3, 1936.

"On Life and Film," *Films in Review* (New York), October, 1952.

"Acting in Film and Theatre," *Film Culture* (New York), No. 5–6, Winter, 1955.

"More Light," *Sight & Sound* (London), Autumn, 1955.

"Plus de Lumière," *Cahiers du Cinéma* (Paris), Oct.–Nov., 1956.

"Le Jeu au Théâtre et au Cinéma," *Cahiers du Cinéma* (Paris), Noël, 1956.

"Créer avec l'oeil," *L'Art du Cinéma* par Pierre Lherminier, Éditions Seghers (Paris), 1960.

"Del Estetismo a la Filosofia," *Gaceto del Festival Mar del Plata,* March 21, 1963.

"A Taste for Celluloid," *Films and Filming* (London), July, 1963.

"The Von Sternberg Principle," *Esquire* (New York), October, 1963.

II. WRITINGS ABOUT STERNBERG

Books

Josef von Sternberg, *The Filmcritic*, Tokyo. (The entire issue of 108 pp. was given over to a critical study of his work.) Part One—1928; Part Two—1933.

The Films of Josef von Sternberg, by Andrew Sarris, Museum of Modern Art, New York, 1966.

Josef von Sternberg/Dokumentation/Eine Darstellung, Verband der Deutschen Filmclubs E.V., Mannheim, 1966.

l'Ange Bleu (Screenplay), *L'Avant-Scène du Cinéma*, No. 57, Paris, March, 1966.

Josef von Sternberg, by Herman G. Weinberg, Éditions Seghers, Paris, 1966.

The Celluloid Sacrifice by Alexander Walker (Chapter 4), Hawthorn Books Inc., New York, 1967.

Interviews

Jean-Claude Bellanger, Dennis Freppel, Bertrand Tavernier, Interview de Josef von Sternberg, *Cinéma 61* (Paris), No. 54, March 1961.

Peter Bogdanovich, Encounter with Josef von Sternberg, *Movie* (London), No. 13, Summer, 1965.

Kevin Brownlow, Sternberg, *Film* (London), Spring 1966.

Felix Bucher, Interview mit Josef von Sternberg, *Film Magazin*, No. 14, 1960.

Serge Daney, Jean-Louis Noames, Recontres avec un solitaire, *Cahiers du Cinéma* (Paris), No. 168, July 1965.

Vitus B. Dröscher, Der Weg zur absoluten Filmkunst—Gesprach mit Josef von Sternberg, *Frankfurter Rundschau*, Dec. 17, 1960.

Philippe Esnault, Michèle Firk, Entretien avec Josef von Sternberg, *Positif* (Paris), No. 37–38, Jan. 1961, March 1961.

Manfred Georg, Eine Begegnung mit Josef von Sternberg, *Die Neue Zeitung*, No. 71, March 25, 1954.

Erich Krünes, Erstes Interview mit Josef von Sternberg, *Film-Magazin* (Berlin), Aug. 25, 1925.

F. A. Macklin, Interview with Josef von Sternberg, *Film Heritage* (Dayton, Ohio), Winter 1965–66.

John Nugent, Total Recall, *Newsweek*, March 29, 1965.

John Pankake, Sternberg at 70, *Films in Review*, May 1964.

Bert Reisfeld, Gespräche mit Josef von Sternberg, *Stuttgarter Zeitung*, Aug. 21, 1959; A Taste for Celluloid, *Films and Filming* (London), July 1963; Le Montreur d'ombres: Déclarations de Josef von Sternberg, *Cahiers du Cinéma* (Paris), No. 168, July 1965; Interview with Sternberg, *Cinema 61* (Paris), No. 54, March, 1961.

Articles

"The Salvation Hunters,"* *The Director* (Hollywood), Dec. 1924.

E.E.B.: "The Luck of von Sternberg," *Picture Goer* (London), January, 1925.

Jim Tully: "Josef von Sternberg," *Vanity Fair* (New York), July, 1928.

Robert Desnos: "Cinéma d'Avant-Garde," *Documents No. 7* (Paris), 1929.

Jean Lenauer: "Dix Jours à Berlin," *La Revue du Cinéma* (Paris), June, 1930.

Jan & Cora Gordon: "Star-Dust in Hollywood" (Edinburgh), 1930.

Louis Chavance: "Le Cas de Josef von Sternberg," *La Revue du Cinéma*, July 1930.

———: "Le Calvaire de Lena X," *ibid*.

Jacques Spitz: "L'Ange Bleu," *La Revue du Cinéma*, October, 1930.

Heinrich Mann: "Le Prof. Unrat," Chapter 1, *La Revue du Cinéma*, December, 1930.

M. Gibbons: "Sternberg," *Film Mercury*, January 2, 1931.

Jean Lasserre: "La vie brûlante de Marlene Dietrich," *Nouvelle Librairie Française* (Paris), 1931.

* Sternberg's first review.

William Ortoni: "Hollywood Has Nothing to Learn," *Atlantic Monthly* (New York), June, 1931.

Henry F. Pringle: "Profile of Josef von Sternberg," *The New Yorker* (New York), March 28, 1931.

Denis Marion: "Un Éthique du Film," *La Revue du Cinéma* (Paris), January, 1931.

Heinrich Mann: "Le Professeur Unrat," (Excerpts), *La Revue du Cinéma* (Paris), December, 1930, January–February, 1931.

Germaine Decaris: "Le Calvaire de Lena X," *Le Soir* (Paris), June 27, 1931.

Robert E. Sherwood: "Shanghai Express" *Hollywood Spectator*, March 1932.

Jean Talky: "Marlene Dietrich, femme enigme," *Nilsson* (Paris), 1932.

Ron Landau-London: "Begegnungen mit amerikanischen Titanen," *Der Ouerschnitt* (Berlin), August, 1932.

"Marlene, hallucinante obsession de Sternberg," *Pour Vous* (Paris), January 12, 1933.

Rudolf Arnheim: "Josef von Sternberg," *Scenario* (Rome), No. 2, 1934.

H.S.: "Von Sternberg als Absolutist," *Filmliga* (Holland), August, 1934.

Andre Sennwald: "J.v.S.—Stylist," *New York Times*, September, 23, 1934.

Andre Armandy: "L'Imperatrice Rouge," *La Revue du Paris*, November 1, 1934.

Arne Bornebusch: "De lever Ett Rikt Livt" (Stockholm), 1935.

Alberto Consiglio: "Attore o regista?" *Cinema* (Rome), No. 1, 1936.

Charles Graves: *"Celebrities in Cameo, No. 50—Joseph von Sternberg,"* *The Bystander* (London), December 9, 1936.

"Marlene Speaks," *Daily Sketch* (London), December 19, 1936.

A. E. Mackenzie: "The Leonardo of the Lenses," *Life and Letters Today* (London), Spring, 1936.

"The Man Who Knows 20,000,000 Minds," *Hong Kong Daily Press*, September 19, 1936.

Eric H. Rideout: *The American Film* (London), 1937.

Pasinetti & Puccini: *La Regia* (Venice), 1943.

John Grierson: "Grierson on Documentary" (London), 1946.
(Pub: Collins).

Roberto Paolella: "Grandezza i decadenza di J.v.S.," *Cinema*
(Milan), No. 26, 1946.

Robert Florey: "Ma carriere à Hollywood," *Hollywood,
d'Hier et d'Aujourd'hui* (Ed. Prisma, Paris), 1948.

Curtis Harrington: "An Index to the Films of Josef von
Sternberg" (Edited by Herman G. Weinberg), Index
Series, No. 17, *The British Film Institute* (London),
February, 1949.

Curtis Harrington: "The Dangerous Compromise," *The Hollywood Quarterly* (Berkeley, Cal.), Vol. 3, No. 4, 1949.

Herman G. Weinberg: "Director's Return," *New York Times*,
Nov. 6, 1949.

Robert Florey: "Escape" (The Exquisite Sinner), *Cinémonde*
(Paris), February 7, 1949.

"A Native Returns," *New York Times*, September 10, 1950.

Jorge Luis Borges: Prologue, *La Muerte y la Brujula* (Buenos
Aires) 1951.

Curtis Harrington: "Josef von Sternberg," *Cahiers du Cinéma*
(Paris), October–November, 1951.

Leslie Frewin: "The Blonde Venus," *Roy Publishers* (New
York), 1953.

Giovanni Scognamillo: "Sternberg, le donne e i gangsters,"
Bianco e Nero (Rome), November–December, 1954.

Guido Cincotti: "Filmografia di von Sternberg," *Bianco e
Nero* (Rome), No. 11–12, 1954.

"Hollywood and Von Sternberg," *New York Post*, January
26, 1956.

Philippe Demonsablon: "Un coeur mis à nu," *Cahiers du
Cinéma* (Paris), April, 1956.

Curt Riess: "Unternehme 'Blauer Engel'" *Das Gab's Nur
Einmal*, Hamburg (Germany), 1956.

Andre Labarthe: "Un metteur en scène baudelairien," *Cahiers
du Cinéma* (Paris), April, 1956.

Ado Kyrou: "Josef von Sternberg" (in *Amour-Érotisme et
Cinéma*), Le Terrain Vague, Paris, 1957.

Gert Wolfram: *Der Sex-Appeal* (Munich), 1957.

"Josef von Sternberg," Kultur Fahrplan (Berlin), 1958.

Kirk Bond: "Joseph von Sternberg Revisited," *Film Courier*
(New York), Summer, 1959.

Herbert G. Luft: "Erich Pommer, Part II," *Films in Review* (New York), November, 1959.

Richard Griffith: "Marlene Dietrich—Image and Legend," Monograph, *Museum of Modern Art* (New York), 1959.

Giulio Cesare Castello and Claudio Bertieri: "The Devil Is a Woman," *Venezia 1932–1939 Filmografia Critica, Bianco e Nero* (Rome), August–September, 1959.

Henri Agel: "Josef von Sternberg," *Les Grandes Cinéastes* (Paris), 1959.

"The Blue Angel," *La Razon* (Caracas), April 3, 1960.

Franco Berutti: "La seconda giovinezza del regista che ha inventato Marlene Dietrich," Venice, 1960.

"Omaggio à Josef von Sternberg," *Festival Bulletin—Locarno*, 1960.

L. KN.: "Josef von Sternberg," *Neues Oesterreich* (Vienna), April 19, 1960.

"Josef von Sternberg," Revista bimestrial de Cinema (Sao Paulo) September, 1960.

"Der Schoepfer des *Blauen Engels*," *Der Kurier* (Berlin), June 28, 1960.

"Joseph: Figura Central de la IV Reseña," *El Grafico* (Acapulco), November 22, 1961.

Ortiz Gonzalez: "Primer Encuentro con el Gran Realizador Aleman—Josef von Sternberg," *Cine Mundial* (Mexico, DF), November 22, 1961.

Octavio Albee: "Canas de Josef von Sternberg," *Cine Mundial* (Mexico, DF), November 30, 1961.

"Sternberg da en el Blanco," *Cine Mundial* (Mexico, DF), December 3, 1962.

"Josef von Sternberg," *Wer ist Wer*, Arani Verlag (Berlin), 1962.

Herman G. Weinberg: "The Lost Films" (Part One), *Sight and Sound* (London), August, 1962.

Jean Douchet: "Sternberg," *Cahiers du Cinéma* (Paris), No. 137, November, 1962.

S. M. Eisenstein: *"Erinnerungen"* (Die Arche Verlag) (Zürich), 1963.

H. Alsina Thevenet: "Josef von Sternberg," *Tiempo de Cine* (Buenos Aires), October–November, 1963.

Walter Khouri: "Filmografia de J.V.S.," *Tiempo de Cine* (Buenos Aires), October–November, 1963.

Carlos Ferreira: "Cineatalya," *La Capital* (Mar del Plata), March 23, 1963.

Ado Kyrou: "Sternberg et Marlène" in *Le Surrealism au Cinéma* (Paris), 1963.

"The Devil Is a Woman & Anatahan," *Protocole du Troisieme Congres International du Cinéma Indépendant,*" SIDOC (*Lausanne*), August 25, 1963—September 1, 1963.

"Von Sternberg—del estetismo a la filosofia," *Gaceta del Festival* (Mar del Plata), March 21, 1963.

"Josef von Sternberg," *El Tiempo* (Bogota), March 24, 1963.

Herbert G. Luft: "J.V.S.—A Study," *Film Journal* (Melbourne) No. 24, December 1964.

Jack Smith: "A Belated Appreciation of Von Sternberg," *Film Culture*, No. 31 (New York), Winter 1963–64.

Al Milgrom: "The Cinema of J.v.S."—Symposium, University of Minnesota, 1964.

Patrick Brion: "Filmographie de Josef von Sternberg," *Cahiers du Cinéma* (Paris), No. 168, July, 1965.

O. O. Green: "Six Films of Josef von Sternberg," *Movie* (London), No. 13, 1965.

Elliott Stein: "Fun in a Chinese Laundry," *Sight & Sound* (London), Autumn 1965.

Herman G. Weinberg: "Sternberg & Stroheim" (letter), *Sight & Sound* (London), Winter 1965–66.

"V.S.—Puppe für Bauchredner," *Der Spiegel*, April 21, 1965.

"Josef von Sternberg ou le cinéma de l'enthousiasme," *Cahiers du Cinéma* (Paris), No. 168, July, 1965.

Ulrich Gregor: "Der Blaue Engel," *Filmkritik* (Frankfurt A.M.), No. 4, April, 1965.

Michel Cournot: "Une cinématique du rêve," *Le Nouvel Observateur* (Paris), February 23, 1966.

Michel Ciment: "Fun in a Chinese Laundry," *Positif* (Paris), No. 75, May 1966.

Bernard Eisenschitz: "L'Oeuvre de Josef von Sternberg," *L'Avant-Scene du Cinéma* (Paris), No. 57, March 1966.

Ado Kyrou: "Sternberg, avant, pendant, après Marlene," *Positif* (Paris), No. 75, May 1966.

Herbert G. Luft: "Josef von Sternberg," *Filmkunst* (Vienna), No. 45, 1966.

Claudio Rispoli: "Il Labirinto sentimentale di Sternberg," *Filmcritica*, No. 166, April, 1966.

Albert Winblad: "Josef von Sternberg," *Kosmorama* (Copenhagen), No. 73, February, 1966.

Ulrich von Thuna: "Ueber die Modernität bei Josef von Sternberg," *Neu Zürcher Zeitung* (Zürich), June 11, 1966.

Herman G. Weinberg: "Fun in a Chinese Laundry" (Review), *Film Heritage* (Univ. of Dayton), May, 1966.

Kirk Bond: "Josef von Sternberg: Three Books," *Film Comment* (New York), Vol. 4, No. 2, 1967.

"Joseph von Sternberg"—*Chaplin 68–70* (Stockholm), December, 1966, February, 1967.

Although this is only a partial listing, it should be stated that a large number of additional articles appeared on Sternberg in late 1966 and early in 1967 in Mannheim, Lyons, Paris, London, Algiers, Oran, Tlemco, Stockholm, Uppsala, Lund, Copenhagen, and Sydney, as a result of his visits to those places.

HERMAN G. WEINBERG was born in New York City in 1908. After attending the Institute of Musical Art where he studied the violin under Louis Svecenski, preparing for a concert career, he changed his mind and entered the field of motion pictures, first scoring foreign films at the Fifth Avenue Playhouse, then subtitling them when sound came in. Since then he has provided the screen captions for over 400 French, German, Italian, etc., pictures. Beginning with *Close-Up* in 1928, he has contributed articles on the aesthetics of the cinema to most of the leading film journals throughout the world, has lectured extensively on this subject in universities in the United States and Canada, inaugurated the Index Series on directors for the British Film Institute as well as a column, *Coffee, Brandy and Cigars*, now in its seventeenth year (and currently appearing in *Film Culture* magazine), comprising "notes for an as yet unwritten history of the cinema." In 1960–61 he served as a juror at the San Francisco and Vancouver International Film Festivals and in 1964 mounted an elaborate exhibition, "Homage to Erich von Stroheim," at the Montreal International Film Festival. The following year he delivered a memorial address on Stroheim at the New York Film Festival and in 1966 at the Canadian Film Institute. He translated and edited the American editions of *50 Years of Italian Cinema* and *50 Years of Ballet and Opera in Italy* and has contributed to many anthologies on the film here and abroad. He was for ten years American Correspondent for *Sight & Sound* (London) and served in a similar capacity for *Cahiers du Cinéma* (Paris), among other film periodicals. His short film, *Autumn Fire*, an early classic of the first American *avant-garde*, is now in the collections of most of the principal film museums here and abroad. He has been "profiled" in *The New Yorker's* "Talk of the Town" and in *Esquire* and has been working on a *"magnum opus," Sin and Cinema*, a moral history of the movies, off and on for the past decade. Currently he is preparing a biography of Ernst Lubitsch, to be published by Dutton in the fall of 1968. Since 1960 he has been teaching a course on the history of the motion pictures as an art at The City College in New York.